YOU ARE CREATIVE

Let Your Creativity Bloom

6th Edition

Dr. YKK (Yew Kam Keong Ph.D)

Edited by:
Evelyn Tian

www.mindbloom.net

BALBOA
PRESS
A DIVISION OF HAY HOUSE

1st edition 1st printing – January 1998
1st edition 2nd printing – March 1998
2nd Edition 1st printing – August 2000
2nd Edition 2nd printing – December 2000
2nd Edition 3rd printing – February 2001
2nd Edition 4th printing – June 2001
2nd Edition 5th printing – December 2001
2nd Edition 6th printing – September 2002
2nd Edition 7th printing – March 2004
3rd Edition 1st printing – 2007
3rd Edition 2nd printing – 2009
3rd Edition 3rd printing – January 2011
4th Edition 1st printing – July 2011
5th Edition – June 2012
6th Edition – Jan 2013

Balboa Press books may be ordered through booksellers or by contacting:

Balboa Press
A Division of Hay House
1663 Liberty Drive
Bloomington, IN 47403
www.balboapress.com.au
1-(877) 407-4847

ISBN: 978-1-4525-0842-9 (sc)
ISBN: 978-1-4525-0847-4 (e)

Printed in the United States of America

Balboa Press rev. date: 12/26/2012

GLOBAL ENDORSEMENTS

I first came across Dr.YKK's book at the Malaysian Embassy in Zagreb, Croatia. The book was so absorbing that I just couldn't put it down. It was so mind-opening and insightful, making a tremendous impact on me. After reading the book, I resolved to meet the author. I travelled all the way from Zagreb to Kuala Lumpur to meet him.

My conversation with him was absolutely scintillating. Knowing that the book will benefit the people of my country, Croatia. I managed to convince him to publish his book in Croatia. I offered to translate the book for him as well as to get a publisher for his book in both Croatia and Slovenia. My efforts paid off. Today, I'm glad to report that Dr.YKK's book has been published both in Croatian and Slovenian languages.

Branka Lucaric
English-to-Croatian Translator
Croatia

"YKK's book is great for Creative Intelligence. Creative thinking complements and enhances IQ. I would strongly recommend this book to all Mensa members as an essential tool to take their already high IQ and couple it to a greater level of creativity."

Dave Remine
Mensa International Chairman, UK

The insights in here will wow and expand your creativity.

Mark Victor Hansen
Best-selling co-author of the
Chicken Soup for the Soul series of books, USA

Yew Kam Keong's book is practical wisdom from the East. It'll show you how to move ahead and create endless possibilities!

Dr. Robert Schuller
Best-selling author of: "Move Ahead with
Possibility Thinking", USA

DR. YKK

To be a great salesperson you need great ideas. This is a great book for getting great ideas.

Joe Girard Greatest Retail Salesman in the World, USA
(Certified by The Guinness Book of World Records)

The book bubbles with contagious enthusiasm and will inspire many people to reach new heights in the way that they approach their studies or work . . . . We will be offering the book to students who undertake such projects with CSIRO Education Programs and members of CSIRO's Double Helix Science Club.

Ross Kingsland
Manager, Education Programs CSIRO Australia

"YOU ARE CREATIVE" challenges us to dare to think the unthinkable. Only then can we help our companies, schools and communities to grow and prosper.

Prof. Fred M.B. Amram
University of Minnesota, U.S.A

Read this book and risk awakening the awesome creativity giant within you. A must-read book for individuals who attend any of my seminars—people who are highly motivated for success.

Gerry Robert
International best-selling Author, Canada

Creativity is about life. This is a book of life.

Pete Crofts
Founder of Humourversity, Australia

Human creativity is the foundation of all human progress. This book stimulates creativity in people of all ages and backgrounds.

Dr. Niels Wiedenhof
Research Scientist, Netherlands

A truly inspirational book on innovation and creativity . . . A single idea from this book could revolutionize your life.

Xenophon Angelelides
International Motivational Speaker, Greece

YOU ARE CREATIVE challenges readers to shake off stale thinking habits . . . Office supervisors ought to be made to study this book before they start to exercise their authority. If they absorb its wisdom, they will avoid acquiring the habit of snubbing staff who proffer fresh ideas.

Penelope MacLachlan
Editor, Mensa International Journal, UK

YKK reminds us of the fundamental truth—that all progress comes from, a playful and inventive state of mind—the true nature and brilliance of a little child. In a conforming world, where we often face fatalism and despair, the greatest need is for new and different solutions, for joy and optimism. YKK embodies this in himself, and in his intelligent and eclectic writings, making creativity part of everyday life. With his help, we can help our children keep and increase their natural creativity. We also benefit ourselves.

Steve Biddulph
Psychologist and best-selling Author, Australia

Creativity to our human beings is just like having wings to birds. In a simple and entertaining way, YOU ARE CREATIVE dramatically makes you build creativity in yourself which can make your life more exciting and meaningful. Read this book; you will find a whole new world inside and outside yourself.

Liu Feng
Educationist, People's Republic of China

I read the book with great interest and my feelings are that people can really learn to put themselves in a mode where they can be more creative than normally by reading your book.

Asger Hoeg
Director, Experimentarium, Denmark

YKK's book is an inspiration to all of us whether young or old. Using basic tools he stirs our curiosity and documents the immense creative abilities of the human mind—resources which are so necessary when facing today's and tomorrow's challenges including the diplomatic world.

Lasse Reimann
Ambassador, Royal Danish Embassy, Malaysia

It amazed me to realize that I was not exerting myself to my full potential. After reading your book I realized that I had skills that I never dream that I ever had. This leads to my discovery of my own creativity and innovativeness. Much has been written about the Knowledge Society. But success in the future will depend not on knowledge alone, but on creativity. This book can help you prepare for the new Creative Society.

Prof. Mitchel Resnick, Media Laboratory
Massachusetts Institute of Technology, USA

This book is a practical guide to expanding personal awareness of the power of creativity. It allows the reader to understand and gain the skills required to expand creative activity and enriching life.

Dr. Stevanne Auerbach
International Toy Expert, USA

YKK has designed a beautiful spark plug for igniting the intellect. May the ensuing creative combustion propel humankind towards the attainment of true genius—our birthright!

Dilip Mukerjea
Best-selling author of Superbrain,
Brainfinity & Braindancing, Singapore

A leader needs to keep an open mind and be receptive to new ideas . . . This is true leadership. This book is a great mind—opener and I strongly recommend leaders and aspiring leaders to read it.

Gregory P. Smith
Author: The New Leader: Bringing Creativity
or Innovation to the Workplace, USA

YKK's book, YOU ARE CREATIVE is a very fun, useful and creative book. It provides immediately useful tools and techniques in a highly creative and practical way. By reading, re-reading and using it in your daily work or personal life you can expand your creativeness and creative thinking skills.

Dr. Robert Alan Black
International Creativity Speaker,
Trainer & Consultant, USA

The book is filled with good ideas to help nurture creativity in children. These are practical, easy suggestions that parents and teachers can use with their children to help them expand their minds. The games, puzzles, and exercises are fun for children and adults too. I am going to use some with my own grandchildren.

Prof Dorothy Singer
Professor, Psychology and Child Study Center;
Co-Director Yale Family Television Research
& Consultation Center, USA

"YOU ARE CREATIVE" is a collection of positive ideas, with the implicit intention of reminding us about the great importance of creativity in human sustainable development.

Eleonora Badilla Saxe
University Of Costa Rica, Costa Rica

This book resembles a treasure chest. There is something for almost every reader, irrespective of whether the reader is a student, a teacher, a grown—up or a parent.

Prof. Chiam Heng Keng
University of Malaya, Malaysia

This book opens our eyes to the world of creativity in a fun and enjoyable way. The vivid and light narration makes the book enjoyable for all levels of society especially students.

Loh Chang Ching
student, Malaysia

"This author, Yew Kam Keong presents a practical proven approach of easy—to-do and yet challenging exercises to unlock our reservoir of intuitive and creative capabilities. Strongly recommended to everyone who aspires to make a difference to the world."

Dato' Lawrence Chan Kum Peng
Executive Chairman,
Personal Development Leadership
Management Corporation, Malaysia

This is a fantastic book! YKK makes us realize that we have a valuable treasure within our own mind. It is now up to us to unlock it! Great work YKK!

Peggy Wong
Global Entrepreneur President/CEO Partners Worldwide
Group of Companies, Malaysia

This book should be on every family's reading list. It stimulates creativity, fun, entertaining, enhance your everyday life, and best of all will strengthen your family bonds. I have benefitted a lot from it and so will the reader.

Kieran Revell
Best-selling author of "Awakening the
Unstoppable Power Within"
Australia

ACTIVATING YOUR CREATIVITY

There are 8 main pathways to activate your creativity.

How we observe

How we listen

How we feel

How we taste

How we smell

How we do our tasks

What we imagine

What we reflect upon

CONTENTS

CREATIVITY EXPLOSION

My head is pounding
Myriad of thoughts
Flashing and whirring
My brain a mechanical instrument
Of Torture!
I cannot bear it,
I groan with frustration.
Like I know the explosion is about to come, Yet the more I focus on it,
The more I delay it.
I let go.
Surrender to the experience of the
moment. Enjoy all life's blessings.
I embrace the sun
Warmth penetrating my being
I whisper to the trees
Caressed by the gentle breeze
Delighting in nature's playground.
And at that moment
Of least expectation,
Flashes of lightning,
Creativity explodes!

Shentelle Gold

Note: *My special thanks to the late Shantelle Gold, a writer, trainer and educator from Australia for dedicating this poem to me.*

30 April 2000

IMPACT OF THIS BOOK ON READERS

"My twenty year old son is cured of his drug addiction," a professional woman in her late forties told me over the phone. I felt happy for her and told her so. But I was totally unprepared for her next words, *"It is all because of your book."*

I never could have imagined that the first edition of this book had such a tremendous impact and touched so many lives. The grateful mother explained to me that her son was hopelessly hooked on drugs. They have checked him into rehabilitation centres and have even engaged traditional and spiritual healers but none of them worked. The family had done all it could but still failed to wean him from this destructive habit. Then, one day the mother got hold of a copy of my book and shared it with her son. Based on the concepts from my book, mother and son used the techniques to generate ideas for business. The son is now highly motivated and manages the business they set up together. His drug habit is effectively cured and he is now thinking of going back to his studies.

Parents have found my book interesting and useful. They passed it to their children to read. Teachers enjoyed reading my book and have used my *Mindxercises* in their classroom teachings. Businessmen have applied some of the techniques in my book and attracted free publicity for their business.

Several budding writers were motivated by my book's success and finally found the courage to complete and to publish their own books.

Alex Leow, the Founder of *Play By Ear* piano course, had the most stupendous wedding ever based on the idea I gave him from this book. It propelled his wedding to be listed in the Malaysian Book of Records. It was the most publicized wedding ever.

> *"Yew Kam Keong (YKK)'s ideas are really powerful, practical and worth a lot of money. The single idea he gave me for my wedding is worth more than US$50,000! He helped make my wedding into*

a major national media event attracting nationwide coverage, put it into the Malaysia Book of Records, gained the attention of the Guinness Book of Records, and attracted many sponsors. Indeed he turned what was to be an ordinary wedding to an unforgettable experience that will be etched into the memory of our guests for a long long time. If you need really great ideas, YKK is the person you should talk to!"

Mr. Alex Leow Proprietor,
Music Talentech Services, Malaysia

This book has continued to touch lives and to equip readers with creative thinking skills. Recently, I got a surprise email from Monika Zec of Macedonia. She said, *"As a new graphic design graduate, I was sooo lost and confused at the beginning but I bought your book a few weeks ago and my life completely changed. It helped me so much."*

Many companies have also made my book as essential reading for their staff. One example is Texas Instruments:

"Our company has bought 100 copies of the book "YOU ARE CREATIVE—Let Your Creativity Bloom" as essential reading for our senior executives as a follow-up to the creativity workshop that YKK has conducted for our organization. His book and his workshop have helped to open up the creative potential of our people's minds."

Mr. Mohd. Azmi Abdullah Manager Training & Organization Effectiveness, Texas Instruments (M) Ltd.

I'm therefore motivated to develop even more resources for my treasured readers, such as audio, video and other publications such as a manual for creativity. So, your feedback is vital to me. Please let me know whether you would be interested in these additional resources and I will work out a very special discount for you as well as to be the first people to be notified when they are ready. The first ten people to respond will get a complimentary copy of the product of their choice. Please send an email to me **drykk@ mindbloom.net** to indicate your preference.

PREFACE TO SIXTH EDITION

I was very gratified that my book has positively impacted families, business executives and entrepreneurs. It has now been published in six languages—English, Mandarin, Malay, Croatian, Slovenian and Macedonian. I expect many editions in other languages to follow.

This English edition has been reprinted 17 times and I have not even started on my marketing yet! Nevertheless, I have received invitations to present talks and conduct creativity and innovation workshops.

This first eBook edition has been updated and substantially improved based on feedback from readers. I would like to particularly single out Lee Say Keng of Singapore who provided several constructive comments, many of which have been incorporated into this new edition. Thanks to Lee and others, I anticipate that this book will touch even more lives than ever before.

My upcoming projects include launching a *Business Innovation Digest* enewsletter to be made available for membership subscription. As my valuable readers, you will be invited for a free subscription if you send an email to DrYKK@mindbloom.net with the title : "Digest".

If you are interested in my original bedtime fairy-tales (see Bloom 9), please email me at DrYKK@mindbloom.net with the title : "*Fairytales*" and I'll email you with an additional five free stories of over 1000 that I have created for my children.

About a year ago, I had an epiphany on innovation. I created a revolutionary 7-Step Innovation system, *Copycat Innovation*™, that fast-tracks innovation by minimizing risk and maximizing gains by leveraging into the awesome power of the internet. Please send me an email DrYKK@mindbloom.net if you are keen to find out more

Experience the thrill of mind unzipping!

Dr. YKK (**Yew** Kam Keong, PhD)
Chief Mind Unzipper
12 Nov 2012

RAINBOW OF CREATIVITY

The following relationship between the rainbow colours and emotions are described by creativity expert, Michael Michaiko. You can take advantage of this relationship by visualizing yourself to be immersed in colour pertaining to the qualities and energies you would like to process.

RED excites the mind and body
ORANGE produces a cheerful state of mind
YELLOW encourages sensitivity
GREEN provides healing and harmony
BLUE eases and relaxes the mind
INDIGO stands for creativity
VIOLET produces revolutionary ideas

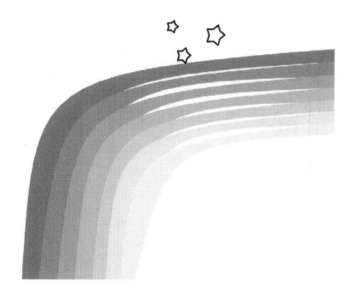

WHY CREATIVITY?

All achievements, all earned riches, have their beginning in an idea.

Napoleon Hill

There is no doubt that creativity is the most important human resource of all. Without creativity, there would be no progress, and we would be forever repeating the same patterns.

Edward de Bono

The world and our civilization have progressed so far due to the power of human creativity. Without creativity, there will be no progress. Without creativity, our civilization as we know it today would have been wiped out by diseases, natural disasters as well as man-made ones. Without creativity we wouldn't be living the quality of life and enjoying the modern amenities of life in the comforts of our homes. Without creativity we wouldn't be able to overcome present and future challenges.

The internet, in particular the social media like Facebook (www.facebook.com), blogs, YouTube (www.youtube.com), Twitter (www.twitter.com) enable us to share our creativity with the world at large. It is also an invaluable tool for us to access the creativity of the best brains in the world.

All of us are creative; we vary only in the extent to which we have developed our creativity potential.

There are three primary reasons why we need to be creative:

1. Joy and Happiness

We get more joy and happiness out of our lives when we harness our power of creativity. The more creative we are, the more we become. We continue to grow; feel more alive; become charged with enthusiasm, thus leading a more meaningful and fulfilling life. Creative effort is also an antidote to worry. And what is worry?—the wrongful use of our imagination.

Creative people love what they do. It is not the hope of achieving fame or amassing wealth that drives them; rather, it is the opportunity to do the things they love most. They feel an inner glow that exudes a sense of happiness.

We are most creative during our childhood days (see Bloom 2). This stage is also our happiest. Studies have shown that on the average the little child laughs about 400 times a day whereas the average adult laughs only 15 times per day.

Capitalizing on creativity promotes a positive outlook and sense of well—being. That boosts the immune system, which keeps us healthy. A healthy person is a happier person.

According to a Reuter's report, creative people tend to lead a more active sex life, which researchers said was no coincidence. Their creativity seems to act like a sexual magnet. A good example is the famous artist Pablo Picasso.

A zest for life, energy, along with sexual desire, these are all qualities of those who embrace Creativity.

Few people personify happiness through creativity better than the late Walt Disney. Disney's creations of fantasy cartoon characters such as *Mickey Mouse, Donald Duck, and Goofy,* along with his Fun-theme parks, *Disneyland* and *Disney World,* bring joy and happiness to millions of people today. What a legacy he left.

As Alice Walker says: *"Helped are those who create anything at all, for they shall relive the thrill of their own conception".*

Walt Disney

It's to be an adult like we are now and to look back through the windows of memory, remembering the time when we were little children, but it's even more exciting to know that we 'became' the kind of people we dreamed about as children. This is called fulfillment.

Walt Disney

Former US President, Franklin D. Roosevelt has this to say: "*Happiness is not in the mere possession of money; it lies in the joy of achievement, in the thrill of creative effort.*"

So what is the second important reason we need to be creative?

2. Survival and Progress

The human race has survived despite incessant threats to its existence through the application of its Creativity. Without it, we'd be dead as the proverbial Dodo. There might be other names for it, such as adaptability, innovation, inventiveness and the like, but call it what you may, in humankind, all of this is *Creativity*.

This fact was borne out by research conducted by Prof. E. Paul Torrance. Torrance was assigned by the US Air Force, early in the Korean War, to develop a training program that would prepare U.S. pilots and their crews to survive in war conditions. This included such situations as being shot down at sea, coming down in the jungle—or even behind enemy lines. After extensive research, Torrance was survival was something that no program at that time had ever taught—Creativity!

In the TV series "McGyver", the hero McGyver always manages to escape from dangerous and almost impossible situations by using his creative imagination. He survives by finding new uses for the things that he has at hand, and adapting them as his escape tools.

In a landmark study of over seven hundred nuns, David Snowdon, Professor of Neurology at the University of Kentucky's College of Medicine, USA, found that there was an 80% correlation between Creativity and the absence of Alzheimer's disease in these nuns in old age. Eighty percent! The march of Alzheimer's seems to be stymied by an active mind.

We humans are the only organism that is able to modify our living environment through technology. Without creativity, no technology is possible. We have progressed thus far with our technology through applying our creativity.

E. Paul Torrance

"Creative problem solving is the only means of survival whenever a person is faced with a life or death situation for which he has no known or practiced solution."

"Every time we are faced with a situation for which here is no given solution we must use creative thinking."

E. Paul Torrance

Let us move on to our third important reason we need to be creative. I'm sure it'll draw your interest.

3. Wealth Creation

The United States of America, still recognized as the most powerful economy in the world, relies on ideas as its main source of foreign exchange income. True. A staggering 42 percent of US exports are ideas, ideas in the form of music, software, books and a plethora of other intellectual capital. Just think of Hollywood, its influence and sales over the years.

The legendary, "El Dorado" of the American Wild West where gold is plentiful, does exist. However, El Dorado is not a place. It is a state of mind. *Ideas* are the true gold of El Dorado.

With the advent of the Internet, we've progressed from the *Knowledge Economy* to the *Creative Economy*. Today, knowledge is accessible to everyone with the click of a mouse-button. Wealth creation is about adding value to this knowledge. And how do we do this? We do it through our creativity. An organization's greatest asset is no longer about physical possession of buildings and machinery. It now stems from the collective creativity of its people.

For instance, founded by Andrew Mason became the fastest growing company in the history of the world. Barely three years old, it rejected a $6 billion takeover bid by Google in 2011.During the filing of its IPO (Initial Public Offering), Groupon was estimated to be worth as much as $30 billion! Other examples include :The purchase of internet telephone company *Skype Technologies* for $2.6 billion by the largest online auction site eBay and Google's acquisition of the No. 1 Internet video sharing Website *YouTube Inc.* for $1.65 billion.

The costs of the physical assets of these two takeovers are almost negligible compared to their systems' creativity values. Creativity is what counts today. And creativity is what will count for a long, long time to come—if not forever—in the advancement of human accomplishment.

We are paying more and more for creativity and imagination and less and less for the materials for the things that we buy. Just consider computer software on compact disks (CDs). The material cost for a blank CD is less than $1.00, yet the CD's software may cost $50,000 or more. The material cost is insignificant. What we are paying for is not the material but the *imagination* contained within the software. That is why, Bill Gates, the wealthiest man in the world, got rich. He acquired his millions by selling to us the imagination of his people.

> *Microsoft is a company that manages imagination.*
>
> Bill Gates

In the business magazine, *Forbes,* of the 2007 ranking of the *World's Richest People*, Bill Gates retained his title as the world's richest person for the *13th straight year*. From 2008 to 2010, he retained his ranking as the top three richest men He did it by selling imagination (software) to the world. Likewise, many on the Fortune—under 40 ranking in 2010 (annual list of the forty richest self-made Americans under the age of forty) created their enormous wealth over a short time by leveraging their creativity over the internet. More than ever before, wealth creation depends on our ability to utilize our creativity and imagination.

Bill Gates

We used tools in the past to leverage our muscles. We use tools today to leverage our minds.

Bill Gates

However, wealth-creation is much more than just software and the World—wide Web. In the 20th century, most business empires were built on a single creative concept—just one idea.

General Motors became the world's largest corporation by introducing the concept of *installment payment* for car purchases. *CNN* became the most popular global TV network by introducing the new concept of *24 hour news*. *Federal Express* (FedEx) made its fortune by introducing the innovative concept of *overnight delivery*. *Coca Cola* became the world's most popular and best-selling drink by bottling it.

Have those three reasons been enough to convince you of the importance of creativity in our lives? Let's look at this a bit more . . .

Talking about tools to leverage our minds, I came across two amazing and revolutionary soft-ware applications for programming microchips. They are: *Core chart* and *ezCircuit* (see details at http://www.elabtronics. com). Without any knowledge of programming at all, I was able to program a micro-controller after only three hours of instruction! No wonder, the

Australian Anthill business magazine (www.australiananthill.com) in its Feb 2007 issue labeled them as a *Disruptive Technologies*.

The 21st century provides the greatest opportunity to leverage creativity on the internet. The Founder and CEO of the social networking site *Facebook*, Mark Zuckerberg, attracted over 800 million members at the time of writing, making him a fabulously rich man. He was named the *"Time Man of the Year 2010"* on 15th December 2010. He is the youngest since Charles Lindbergh was named as the first Time Man of the Year in 1927.

4. Experts Can Be Wrong!

- *"The phonograph . . . is not of any commercial value."*
  Thomas Edison remarking on his own invention, 1880
- *"Man will not fly for fifty years."*
  Wilbur Wright to his brother Orville, in 1901 (Two years later Wilbur and Orville Wright did fly)
- *"There is no likelihood man can ever tap the power of the atom."*
  Robert Millikan, Nobel Prize winner in Physics, 1920
  (Are you getting the message here? Even those directly involved in a project cannot always accurately envisage its eventual outcome. This is why it pays to always keep an open mind.)
- *"Who the hell wants to hear actors talk?"*
  Harry Warner, Warner Brothers Pictures, 1927
- *"I think there is a world market for about five computers."*
  Thomas J. Watson, Chairman of IBM, 1943
- *"Computers in the future may weigh no more than 1.5 tons."*
  Popular Mechanics, 1949
- *"Space travel is utter bilge."*
  Dr. Richard van der Riet Wooley, British Astronomer Royal, 1956
  (Two years later, the Soviet Union launched the first satellite and Dr. Wooley was named to a British Commission to advise the government on space research)
- *"Groups with guitars are on their way out."*
  Decca Records turning down the Beatles, 1962
  (The Beatles went on to become the most famous international pop group in the 1960's)

- *"There is no reason for any individual to have a computer in their home."*
  Ken Olsen, President of Digital Equipment Corp., 1977
- *"640K ought to be enough for anybody"*
  Bill Gates, Chairman of Microsoft, 1981
  (Nowadays, a 250 Gigabyte (1 Gigabyte = 1 million Kbyte) laptop is common place and external hard-drives are available for 2 Terabyte (1 terabyte=1000Gigabyte)
- *"ZAP! How the Year 2000 Bug Will Hurt the Economy"*
  (Business Week cover story on the Y2K Bug, which started the whole Y2K hysteria in 1998)

5. You Don't Need to be An Expert to Create Breakthroughs!

Everything of importance has been seen by someone who did not discover it.
Alfred North Whitehead

The world is but canvas to our imaginations.
Henry David Thoreau

- The first frequency hopping anti-jamming submarine communication system was invented by Hedwig Kiesler Markey, a Hollywood actress (known under her actress name as Hedy Lamarr. You may remember her from the 1950s film 'Sampson and Delilah' with Victor Mature)
- The cash register was invented by Jake Ritty, a restaurant bar owner.
- The electric motor was invented by Thomas Davenport, a blacksmith.
- The Kodak camera was invented by George Eastman, a bank clerk.
- The first ballpoint pen was invented by Laszlo Biro, a Hungarian journalist.

Okay, let us see if we can enhance our own creativity here with a few 'mind—stretchers.'

Mindxercise 1.1 Guess Their Professions

Guess the professions of the people making the breakthroughs by matching the column on the left with the correct answers on the right.

Breakthroughs	Professions
1. The Lithograph used in the printing industry was invented by Alois Senefelder	A. Playwright
3. The pneumatic tyre was invented by John Boyd Dunlop.	C. Bicycle repairman
4. The first flying airplane was invented by the Wright Brothers.	D. Portrait painter
5. The telegraph and Morse Code was invented by Samuel Morse.	E. Veterinarian
6. The telephone automatic switching system was invented by Almond B. Strowger	F. Bridge builder

Rejection Could Indicate That Your Idea Has Great Potential

Great spirits have always encountered violent opposition from mediocre minds.

Albert Einstein

An idea's worth is directly proportional to the opposition created.

Robert Townsend

- The series of books on Harry Potter written by JK Rowling was rejected by 12 publishers including major publishing houses like Penguin, TransWorld and Harper Collins. She went on to become a billionaire and the richest author who ever lived.
- EDS founder, H. Ross Perot who sold his company in 1984 to General Motors for US$2.5 billion was rejected by IBM when he proposed to create a service organization that would design, install and operate electronic data processing systems on a fixed contract basis.

- Federal Express founder Fred Smith's paper proposing reliable overnight delivery service got only a "C" grade from his Yale University professor who dismissed the idea as not feasible.
- The million copies international best-selling "Chicken Soup for the Soul" book by Mark Victor Hansen and Jack Canfield was rejected by 33 publishers before they found a publisher to publish their book.
- Kentucky Fried Chicken founder Col. Harland Sanders method of frying chicken was rejected by more than 1000 restaurants before he found success.
- Gillette Safety Razor founder, King C. Gillette, tried in vain for six years to raise money to produce his razor shaving blade. It was only in 1901 that he managed to persuade some friends to raise $5000 to form a company.
- Apple Computer Inc. founders Steve Jobs and Steve Wozniak were rejected by both Atari and Hewlett-Packard when they tried to get the two companies interested in their personal computer project.
- Walt Disney, the founder of Disneyland and the creator of Disney animation movies was fired by a newspaper editor for lack of ideas.
- Albert Einstein did not speak until he was four years old and didn't read until he was seven. His teacher described him as "mentally slow, unsociable and adrift forever in his foolish dreams." He was expelled and was refused admittance to the Zurich Polytechnic School.
- Beethoven, the great musician was branded as hopeless by his teacher. He handled the violin awkwardly and preferred playing his own compositions instead of improving his technique.
- Thomas Edison, one of the greatest inventors who ever lived and held 1093 patents, was constantly scolded by his teacher as being too stupid to learn anything.

The Greatest Secret About Creativity

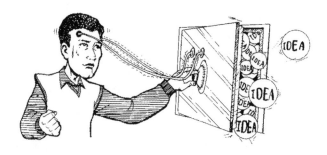

"The secret to creativity is knowing how to hide your sources."
Albert Einstein

After an intensive and extensive study on creativity in which researchers interviewed thousands of creative people on their background, age, sex, occupation, etc., they came to a conclusion which reveals the greatest secret about creativity. This is the secret which, when revealed to you, will make you aware that you could become a creative person if you choose to be one.

In his book, *Creativity: Flow and the Psychology of Discovery and Invention*, Mihalyi Csikszentmhalyi interviews creative people from many different fields: the arts, mathematics and science, inventors, educators, thinkers, therapists. He concludes that creative people are not people who simply happen to connect with and express their own innate abilities but people who combine their abilities with disciplined practice. They actually invest time in finding and developing their flow experience—through activities which actively nurture this.

To be creative, we need not only to be able to allow our ideas to emerge, but we also need to constantly practice our particular skill, through consistent disciplined practice. We need to combine playfulness with emotional intelligence, nurturing creative freedom and discipline.

Teresa Amabile, a well-known creativity researcher at Harvard Business School has found that there is a strong correlation between creative performance and "intrinsic motivation". When we are working on a task out of passion and personal interest, we are more likely to demonstrate creativity than if we are pursuing the task in order to achieve an extrinsic reward, like money, fame or promotion.

Mindxercise 1.2: The Greatest Secret

To discover this secret, you will need to read this book from cover to cover as *Jig-words** (clues in the form of short phrases) will be given along the way. The *Jig-words** are in italics. There are eight (8) of them all together. Once you have the full set of 8 *Jig-words** all that you need to do is to join them up like a jigsaw puzzle. Fill up the spaces below as you discover each *Jig-word**.

Like the other good things in life, you have to put in some effort but the reward is great—so begin on your joyous and mind stimulating trip to discover the greatest secret about creativity!

*Jig-word** 1

_____

*Jig-word** 2

_____

*Jig-word** 3

_____

*Jig-word** 4

_____

*Jig-word** 5

_____

*Jig-word** 6

_____

*Jig-word** 7

_____

*Jig-word** 8

_____

The Greatest Secret about Creativity is:

_____

_____

_____

_____

_____

RECORD YOUR
CREATIVITY BLOOM HERE

WHAT IS CREATIVITY?

Let us not follow where the path may lead. Let us go instead where there is no path and leave a trail.

Japanese Proverb

The common cliché is "get real". Our watchword will be "get bizarre". Real solutions to problems (true creativity) come from fantasy rather than from the file cabinet in our head.

Fred M. Amram

There are probably hundreds of definitions of creativity. Some are simple, some are light-hearted, some are serious, some are technical and of course some are very complicated. For the purpose of this book, I have chosen this definition:

Creativity is about making connections where none existed before.

Being open-minded, alert, attentive, and willing to give any concept which comes into our heads more than a cursory examination followed by the all-too-common automatic rejection, is essential to the creative process.

We were given the idea. It came from something bigger, more profound and far more knowledgeable than our normal everyday thought patterns. Sometimes that intuitively gathered information might seem ludicrous. If it was—then why did we get it? Sometimes the incongruity might be so great that we can see no link at all. But given a moment of silence, a flash of insight might make it clear. So give it a chance.

If an idea comes, record it straight away. Write it down. Don't trust it to memory, unless it is so simple and so visual you have no possibility of losing it to short-term memory. Writing it down serves several purposes. You are defining or describing in brief the idea you've received, and just as importantly, you are sending a message to your subconscious mind that you are able and willing to take down such messages. Doing this will encourage that unconscious part of your psyche to keep providing good ideas.

What happens when you say something to someone and they ignore you? You try again, perhaps, but with less enthusiasm. They still won't listen? You eventually give up. That part of you that was originally so enthused to give you new and creative ideas will do the same. So, don't ignore it. Don't snub it—encourage it. It wants to help you, so let it. But let us look now at a few brilliant ideas that have come to those who were ready, able, and willing to run with them.

Creative Connections that changed the world!

- Jack Dorsey made a connection between SMS (short messaging service) for mobile phones and the idea of an individual using an SMS service to communicate with a small group to create Twitter (a text-based post posts of up to 140 characters) as a social networking and micro blogging service in 2006.
- Andrew Mason made a connection between the Social Charity site *The Point (www.thepoint.com)* and group discount coupons to create Groupon, the fastest growing company in the history of the world.
- Johann Gutenberg made a connection between a wine press and a coin punch to invent the printing press.
- Pablo Picasso, a famous artist, made a connection between a bicycle handlebar and a bull to create a famous sculpture using the bicycle handlebar as bullhorns.
- Jacques Heim, a French designer, made a connection between beachwear and the tiny Pacific Island of Bikini where the atom bomb was tested to name the world's smallest beachwear that he had designed as the "bikini".

- Sylvan N. Goldman, a supermarket operator, made a connection between his customers struggling to carry all their purchases and two small folding chairs to develop the shopping trolley.
- Christopher Sholes made a connection between piano keys and a writing machine to invent the typewriter.
- Clarence B. Darrow, who was always short of money, made a connection between poor people and people who could imagine that they were rich to invent the game called "Monopoly".
- Ole Evinrude made a connection between the car's petrol engine and a boat to invent the Evinrude, the first commercialized outboard motor for boats.
- Philo Farnsworth, while ploughing his father's field, noticed that the field being ploughed in was a set of parallel lines. He made a connection between the parallel lines and the transmission of a picture line by line to invent television. Philo was only 14 when he got this inspiration.
- Erno Rubik, was stuck with workable internal mechanism for his cube. He was inspired one day in 1974 while he took a walk by the banks of the Danube River. Rubik made a connection between the smooth, polished, rounded stones at the bank and the rounded elements for the center core of the cube to invent the famous Rubik Cube puzzle.
- Mary Phelps Jacob made a connection between two silk handkerchiefs and the need for a comfortable undergarment to invent the first modern brassiere (bra) for women.

All Of Us Are Creative

All of us are creative. We differ only in the degree and scope of our creativity. There is no one person who is creative in all fields of human endeavor, not even Einstein. The only person who, I believe came close is Leonardo da Vinci who excelled in both the arts and in the sciences.

Leonardo is widely considered to be the most diversely talented person ever to have lived. His painting of Mona Lisa, housed in the Louvre Museum in Paris, is considered to be the most famous and most marvelled painting in the world. As self-taught scientist, Leonardo is also revered for his technological ingenuity. He conceptualised the helicopter, structure of the human anatomy, solar power and civil engineering construction well ahead of his time.

Eight Intelligences

Howard Gardner, a well-respected Harvard University professor, believes that all of us possess a combination of different intelligences to varying extents, with one or two being dominant. He came to this conclusion based on his study of people from many different walks of life in everyday circumstances and professions to develop his theory of *Multiple Intelligences*. He defined the first seven intelligences in his book *Frames of Mind* in 1983 and added one more in *Intelligence Reframed* in 1999.

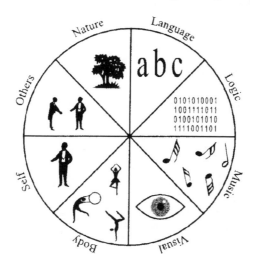

The original *Seven Intelligences* were quickly embraced by both educational institutions and the industry as a learning model for which to understand and teach the differing aspects of human intelligence, learning style, personality and behaviour.

Though he does not isolate a Creative intelligence, creativity is implied in all his original seven intelligences.

No.	Intelligence	Skill/Preferred Learning Style	Career Preference
1	Linguistic	use of the spoken or written language	writers, speakers, trainers, teachers, journalists
2	Logical/ Mathematical	logical and analytical thinking	accountants, engineers, mathematicians, scientists
3	Musical	musical notes or rhythm	musicians, singers, dancers
4	Visual/Spatial	space, colours and designs	designers, artists, architects
5	Bodily/ Kinesthetic	body coordination and movement	athletes, acrobats, stunt people, stage performers
6	Intrapersonal	self-awareness and staying in tune with inner feelings, values, beliefs and thinking processes (emotional intelligence, EQ)	philosophers, researchers, theoreticians
7	Interpersonal	interacting with people(another component of emotional intelligence, EQ, see No. 6 above)	salespersons, politicians, leaders, psychologists
Intelligence No. 8 was added in 1999			
8	Naturalist	affinity for living things	Biologists, environmentalists, naturalists, botanists, gardeners

The question therefore is not : *Are you Creative?* But *How are you Creative? Which of Gardner's Intelligences dominate in you.?* By being aware and focusing on your dominant intelligence, you can speed up your own learning and achieve success in what you set out to do much faster. In the same way, by understanding other people's dominant intelligence, you will be able to establish a much more harmonious relationship with them and be able to guide them along to achieve fulfillment and happiness in their lives.

Dr. Gardner says that our schools and culture focus most of their attention on linguistic and logical-mathematical intelligence and neglect the others. Personally, I think that in our 21st century, the internet and computer games with their multimedia approach are much more conducive to the diverse learning styles of the new generation.

Intelligence Trap

There is a low correlation between creativity and intelligence as measured by I.Q Tests above 120 IQ points. Based on research conducted by Yonsei University in Seoul, Korea, creativity is not related to either intelligence or school achievement. Generally, intelligence is a measure of convergent thinking (coming to a conclusion based on a series of facts) while creativity is about divergent thinking (see many possibilities to an issue at hand).

Of course a certain degree of intelligence (about 120 IQ points) is important for creativity to happen. However, there is a danger of highly intelligent people falling into their own "intelligence trap". The research of Chris Argyris at Harvard has confirmed this phenomenon. He has observed that intelligent, successful professionals tend to make good decisions. They seldom make mistakes. As a result, they have little experience with being wrong and are less inclined to listen to other people's ideas. Thus on the occasions when they are wrong, they don't see it and tend to become very defensive. Being intelligent, they can construct a rational, well-argued case to defend their point of view. Chris terms this response "defensive routines", which is actually a form of the intelligence trap.

Intelligent people are highly creative if they are aware of this "intelligence trap" and keep an open mind. Gifted geniuses have a good combination of intelligence and creative thinking.

However, creativity is not a monopoly of gifted geniuses. All of us are capable of creative work under the right environment and when we are sufficiently inspired. After all, creativity is an activity resulting from the thought processes of ordinary individuals.

Einstein—Mentally Retarded?

When Albert Einstein was interviewed on the source of his creative genius, he was purported to have replied, *"It is because I'm mentally retarded."* Is it possible that one of the greatest geniuses who ever lived was mentally retarded?

Fortunately, Einstein explained what he meant. Einstein had the mind of a child but the brain of a scientist. Like a child, he was constantly asking probing questions which adults regarded as *"silly"* like: *"What will happen if I ride on a light beam?"* Incidentally, it was this question that led to his discovery of his famous *"Theory of Relativity"*.

In essence, Einstein never grew up. He retained his childlike curiosity. That was why he considered himself *"mentally retarded"*. Unlike a child, however, Einstein was able to answer his own questions because he had the knowledge and creativity of a scientist.

Another quality of Einstein was that he imagined in pictures rather than using the language of words in his thinking. Every language carries with it inherent limitations that restrict thinking. For instance, the definition of the word "atom" as an indivisible part of matter restricted thinking about the structure of atoms for many years. Words have limitations. Thinking visually and escaping from our linguistic limitations enriches our imagination.

Therein lies a secret to creativity—maintain the innocent curiosity of a child and imagine in pictures more than words.

Stories Of Creativity

2.1 The Woman Who Made Millions By Connecting Painting With Typing

In the 1950s when the electric typewriter was first introduced to the market, a kind-hearted boss bought one for his secretary. The new electric typewriter fascinated Bette Nesmith, who had to struggle with a mechanical model all along, as it would save her from having sore fingers from pounding the keys.

Bette's joy was short-lived. Being unfamiliar with the soft-touched keys, she made mistake after mistake until her waste-paper basket was full of incorrectly typed letters. She was unable to finish a single letter at the end of the day.

Bette thought hard on ways to overcome the problem but no solutions came. Finally she gave up and switched her thoughts to the reaction of the boss. He had invested a lot on the new typewriter and would be very disappointed if she was unable to work more efficiently. She could even lose her job.

In the midst of her sad thoughts, an idea suddenly flashed into her mind. She remembered that in her art training she had learned to paint over mistakes with a special paint called Gesso. Eureka! That's it!

Bette rushed home to find a tin of white paint and used her small paintbrush to paint over her mistakes. Thus the corrector fluid, Liquid Paper was born. In 1972, she sold the company to the Gillette Corporation for US$50 million!

2.2 Playing Golf Like Tennis?

The Callaway golf club designer was looking for inspiration to design a new golf club that would attract new players to play golf. He went to the driving range of a golf club to observe beginners learning to hit the balls. They were hitting fairly well with the short iron clubs but when they tried to use the long wooden clubs, they missed many shots. He could see the frustration on their faces each time they missed the ball.

The next day, the designer's friend invited him for a game of tennis. His friend remarked that tennis was a much more popular game than golf. When asked why, he replied that it was much easier to hit a small tennis ball with a big racket face than to hit a small golf ball with a small club face.

After the tennis game, the designer pondered over his friend's statement. He felt that more people would take up golf if hitting the golf ball was made as easy as hitting the tennis ball. The inspiration came as he was driving home. He made the connection! Why not make an over-sized golf club head to provide a bigger surface area for hitting the golf ball?

He made a prototype club and handed it over to the novice players for testing at the driving range. Sure enough, the new club added to their enjoyment and their frustrations practically disappeared.

Thus Callaway became the first golf club manufacturer to produce the over-sized golf club head. The "Big Bertha" club was launched in 1990 and became an instant success. The result: not only were new players drawn into the market, but Callaway captured a significant share of the existing players as well.

2.3 Bicycle Inspired Guitar Strings

Dave Myers was an engineer working at W.L Gore, designated by Fastcompany as the most innovative company in America in 2004. Myers' work included helping to invent new kinds of plastic heart implants. One day, while Myers was working on his mountain bike, he coated the gear cables with a thin layer of plastic to make the gears shift more smoothly. His tinkering resulted in Gore's "Ride-On" line of bike cables.

Myers continued with his tinkering of coating cables with plastic for various applications. He experimented with guitar strings for one of his projects. Suddenly, he made a connection. If the coated guitar string can be used for a non-guitar project, why not use it on the guitar itself?

Myers wasn't a guitarist himself, so he sought help from a guitar-playing engineer who understood the frustrations of guitar players with the instrument. The engineer explained that whenever you play a guitar you leave behind on the strings some sweat, body oils, tiny bits of dead skin, and any dirt or soils that were on your hands. This severely affected the sound quality of the guitar.

The plastic coating offered a solution to shield your strings from all these damaging elements. This however, did not solve the problem of maintaining the sound quality. It took the research team three years and with the assistance of 5000 musician testers to perfect the new plastic-coated strings.

The final product is marketed as ELIXIR. The strings are covered with an ultra-thin, space-age polymer tube that contacts the string on the tops of the windings only. This leaves the all important strings above the hollow guitar space free from sound distortion thereby leaving its sound quality intact. It was an astounding success.

You need not be an expert in your field of invention. All you need is a good idea or connection, work on it and then seek the help of experts.

Mindxercise 2: Making the Connection

Below are some connections that were made and which resulted in commercial success. Why not try them yourself? You may not be able to come out with the same connections, but it doesn't matter. *If you* (*Jig-word* 1) can make your own original connections, just one of them may make you rich like Bette Nesmith!

1. What products were made by making the following connections?
    (a) Tooth-picks and cotton
    (b) Car and home
    (c) Chair and wheel
    (d) Perfume spray and car engine
2. The following pairs of words have been combined in perfume advertisements to create the desired impact. Could you do the same?
    (a) Scents and sensation

    (b) Scents and sensual

    (c) Scents and sentimental

3. Study the pattern of the whole numbers from 1 to 100. Look for a simple connection between selected pairs of numbers. Now, using this connection, add the whole numbers 1 to 100 mentally within 10 seconds.

4. Some of the world's famous eating places were created by making connections. Could you figure out the names of the following eating places based on the pairs of ideas below?

    (a) Café bar and Rock Music

    (b) Restaurant and Hollywood stars

    (c) Pizza and fast home delivery

5. What famous world products were created or marketed by making the pairs of connections below:

    (a) Watch and fashion

    (b) Shoes and specific types of sports

    (c) Beer and soft drinks

    (d) Drinking water and luxury

RECORD YOUR
CREATIVITY BLOOM HERE

NON-CREATIVE BEHAVIOUR IS LEARNED

Creativeness is a fundamental characteristic inherent in human beings at birth.

Abraham Maslow

Creativity skills require practice and can be enhanced by teaching.

Paul Torrance

In 1965, futurist George Land and his team developed a test for NASA (National Aeronautics and Space Administration, USA) to select their most creative engineers and scientists for its Space program. The test was highly successful.

In 1968, the test was expanded to 1,600 pre-school young children aged five. The test was repeated to the same children at age 10 and 15. The same test given to 280,000 adults many years later placed their creativity level at only 2% !

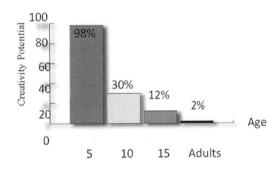

In his book *"Breakpoint and Beyond"*, co-authored by Beth Jarman, Land concluded that *"non-creative behavior is learned"*.

The conclusion is that children are extremely creative, but once they started schooling, their creativity drops tremendously. In school, children are literally taught how not to be creative.

The good news is that through creativity training you can unlearn how not to be creative and be creative again like a child. By reading this book, you have taken a step forward to regain your birth-right and be creative again.

Torrance Test For Creative Thinking

The late Dr. Paul Torrance of the University is widely considered by creativity practitioners to be the father of creativity. He devoted most of his life on a method to quantify creativity. Torrance developed the "Torrance Tests of Creative Thinking" which has universal applications.

His basic four criteria are very useful and could be used to determine whether we have a creative session, whether planning for a holiday at home or at a business meeting.

Frequently, the so-called brainstorming sessions are just routine meetings producing stereotyped ideas. The Torrance Test will help us to determine whether we have a truly creative session.

The 4 criteria for *Torrance Tests of Creative Thinking* are as below:

1. Quantity of Ideas (or *Fluency*)—how many ideas can you come up with?
2. Variety of Ideas (or *Flexibility*)—how many different ideas can you come up with?
3. Uniqueness (or *Originality*)—can you come up with an idea that no one else has?
4. Elaborateness—can you explain or provide details to your idea?

I have simplified and interpreted Torrance Tests my way so that you could apply them easily. My interpretation of each of the four criteria is as below:

Quantity of Ideas

Before you start the session, set a target for the minimum ideas that you intend to get within a specified time-frame. For example, you intend to come out with 25 ideas for a holiday within 15 minutes. If you come out with 25 ideas or more in 15 minutes then you have achieved your first criterion.

Variety of Ideas

Examine the ideas that you have generated and categorise them. For example for your holidays, you could classify them under: picnic, visits to places of interest, overseas, adventure, etc. If you could classify them into different categories, then you have a variety of ideas.

Uniqueness

Look at your ideas under the different categories. Is there one or more that stand out as being different; something new that you have never thought of before? A good test of this uniqueness is whether it creates a strong emotional reaction. Does it create fear, apprehension or excitement? Whatever emotions surface, just proceed to the next stage.

Elaboration

Once you identify the unique idea or ideas, ask the person who suggested the idea to explain it. Listen and do not interrupt until the person has finished the elaboration. Then ask questions to show interest and to have a better understanding. Do not criticize or give any negative comments. The others are encouraged to add their own ideas to the elaboration. If at this stage, nearly everyone gets excited, then most likely you have a winning idea! Repeat this process for the other unique ideas, then select one to implement. Record and keep the unused ideas as may be handy later.

Did you get it? If you do, apply the 4 criteria for *Torrance Tests of Creative Thinking* at your next creative session. Your meeting will be much more lively, exciting and more likely to produce winning ideas!

Mindxercise 3.1: Test Your Creativity Potential

The test below provides only an indication of your personal creativity potential.

Score yourself against each statement. Do not think too long. The best answers are your intuitive feelings that first pop into your mind.

		Low				High
1.	I am creative	1	2	3	4	5
2.	If I think I'm creative, I will be creative	1	2	3	4	5
3.	I like to discover my creativity potential	1	2	3	4	5
4.	I explore new ways of doing things	1	2	3	4	5
5.	I'm willing to take risks in doing things differently	1	2	3	4	5
6.	I yearn to learn outside my scope of work	1	2	3	4	5
7.	I prefer ideas and theories to facts and figures	1	2	3	4	5
8.	I ask lots of questions before giving my response	1	2	3	4	5
9.	I love doing mentally stimulating exercises	1	2	3	4	5
10.	I enjoy jokes and funny cartoons	1	2	3	4	5

Scoring Guide :
  41-50 : Very Creative
  31-40 : Creative
  21-30 : Fairly Creative
  10-20 : Could be More Creative

Mindxercise 3.2: The Power Of Observation

Though knowledge is acquired through all the five senses, the power of observation is most important. The Mindxercises below test your power of observation. Try to observe them in a different way and you will be fascinated by the result.

How many faces do you see?

Young or Old?

Can you see Napoleon on Elba Island?

Can you trust this man?

RECORD YOUR
CREATIVITY BLOOM HERE

FIVE STEPS TO CREATIVITY

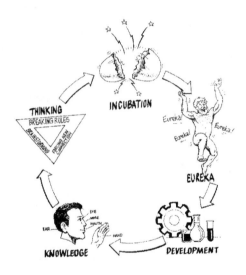

Creative thinking is not a talent; it is a skill that can be learnt. It empowers people by adding strength to their natural abilities which improves teamwork, productivity and where appropriate—profits.

Edward de Bono

The highest creativity occurs in well-organized environments. Poor organization leads to wasted time and confusion. Confused people are not creative people.

Mike Vance

Knowledge :   Acquire diverse knowledge utilizing all the five senses
Thinking :   Think deeply
Incubation :   Relax and do something unrelated to the problem
Eureka! :   I found it! Moment of Inspiration.
Development :   Developing ideas into useful and practical applications

Step 1: Knowledge

Knowledge is being applied to knowledge itself. It is now fast becoming the one factor in production, sidelining both capital and labor.

Peter Drucker

Exposure to wide and varying experience and situations is good for the creation of new ideas.

Hean-Tatt Ong

Creativity is about making connections. Knowledge is the raw material that you can use to make connections. Thus it follows that the more diverse the knowledge that you have, the greater are your chances of making a new connection where none existed before.

Knowledge is not just about the formal education that you have received but rather it is the sum total of all our life-long experiences using our five senses of sight, sound, smell, taste and touch.

Reading and learning about subjects outside your scope of expertise is essential in order to introduce innovation to your work. If you are an engineer by profession for example, you should try to read something different, like poetry, astronomy and other fields totally unrelated to your work. A good way to get out-of-the-box thinking and to come out with really innovative ideas is to get out of routines. Read magazines you have not read before, go to movies which you do not like, try out a new hobby, learn new skills, talk to strangers and be adventurous in trying out new things or experiences.

The fastest and easiest way to acquire knowledge is to read through the Weekend papers. You may forego the news but make sure you read just about everything else in the feature section—sports, science, health, finance, cartoons, etc.

Make it a habit to pick up a magazine with a title that you normally do not read. Reading a different magazine at least once a month will do wonders to your creativity. Select titles of magazines which you have no interest in, for example: Tattooing and you will be amazed at what new knowledge you can discover. Browsing through unfamiliar reading materials while waiting for your business or dental appointments is not only a great way to pass the time but also a unique opportunity to open up new horizons of knowledge that will enrich your creativity.

Strike up a conversation with foreigners wherever and whenever you can. Show a genuine interest in your questions to learn something new about their culture, their way of life, their social and political system, the games they play and any other topic that you have very little or no knowledge of. Curiosity is one of the foundations of creativity.

The more knowledge you accumulate, the greater is the pool of resources you can bring to generate new ideas. Look for knowledge outside your sphere of study or expertise. The creator of Apple computer, Steve Jobs, recounted how modern dancing helped him to relate to movements which enabled him to design computer games when he worked at Atari.

In the case of Bette Nesmith, the inventor of Liquid Paper, her knowledge of art, which she took up as a hobby, enabled her to finally solve her typing problem.

Though there is as yet no concrete scientific evidence, it is generally believed that there is a sixth sense known as intuition. Some refer to intuition as the thinking process of the subconscious mind that draws on experiences that we do not remember. No one knows exactly how it works but many are convinced.

That intuition is the source of true creativity that resides in all of us.

Stories of Creativity

4.1 The Man Who Knows Everything

Once upon a time there lived a very wise man who sold words for a living. Though he charged a great deal for his words, it was well worth the cost as they changed the lives of his clients for the better. The words that he sold were only effective if his client kept the words to himself and tried to figure out their meaning without enlisting anyone's help.

His fame spread far and wide and soon the King heard about him.

The King summoned the wise man to the castle but the man would not come. The King had no choice but to go to him to buy his words. Upon the King's arrival, the man studied the King intently without uttering a word. Finally, he said, "Everything I know!" and charged the King thirty gold pieces for those three words.

The King tried to figure out the hidden meanings behind the three words but was unsuccessful. He pondered over the words for several days and nights. He dared not even consult his closest advisers, as he was well aware that it would invalidate the impact of those words.

One day, the King's regular barber was called to the castle to give him a haircut. While the barber was cutting his hair, the King pondered over the words. Finally, he could no longer control himself and blurted out the words in a loud voice, "Everything I know!" The barber's face turned ashen. He immediately dropped the knife he was using to shave the King's face and knelt before the King.

"Please forgive me for trying to slit your throat as instructed by your brother," the barber cried as he pleaded for his life.

Thus the three words saved the King's life.

What do you think? Do you think that the wise man really knew everything or was it the case of the wise man creatively using his knowledge that there would always be aspirants to the throne?

Mindxercise 4.1: Use Your Knowledge

To solve the following problems, you need to have some knowledge in sports, science and a keen power of observation. Have fun!

1. A woman was filling up her bathtub with hot water when the hot water ran out. She therefore decided to heat some water in a kettle on the kitchen stove in order to add to the water in the bath to raise the temperature to the desired result. After some time, her husband walked in. He told her to stop heating the water on the stove because the more she heated the water, the colder will be her bath. Why?

2. Two girls were playing in a tennis competition. They had to play 5 sets before the match result could be determined. When the final results were announced, each of the girls won three sets. How was this possible?

3. There are 200 players taking part in a singles knock-out tennis competition. Assuming that there were no walkovers, how many matches had to be played to determine the champion?

4. An Anagram is a word or phrase made by rearranging the letters of the same word or phrase into another word or phrase using the same letters. For example: The anagram for "A Decimal Point" is "I'm a Dot in Place". Notice that the anagram has exactly the same letters as the original phrase.

5. Can you explain the following words or phrases in a form of an Anagram?
   (a) Eleven plus two
   (b) The Morse Code
   (c) Desperation

Step 2: Thinking

> *Some people study all their life, and at their death, they have learned everything except to think.*
>
> Domerge

> *Natural resources have dropped out of the competitive equation. In fact, a lack of natural resources may even be an advantage. Because the industries we are competing for—the industries of the future—are all based on brainpower.*
>
> Lester Thurow

Thinking activates the mind to make useful connections to come out with possible solutions to the problem at hand. According to the work of Nobel laureate, Dr. Roger Sperry, the functions of the brain is split into two hemispheres. The left hemisphere deals with Logical Thinking (just remember that L = Logic) whilst the right brain deals with ideas. You need to use both halves of the brain to be able to generate ideas (right brain) and to evaluate and develop the ideas to practical applications (left brain).

Table: Characteristics of Left & Right Brain

Left Brain	Right Brain
Logical	Emotional
Language	Creative
Analytical	Subjective
Objective	Random
Sequential	Rhythm

Another discovery was that the right brain controls the left side of our body and the left brain controls the right side. Therefore any activity that brings about coordination of the left and right side of our body will enhance creativity. Such activities include swimming, dancing, gymnastics and juggling. If you were a right-hander, it would be good to increase the use of your left hand and vice versa for the left—handers.

According to the famous creativity expert, Edward de Bono, there are two types of thinking processes. The first is vertical or convergent thinking. According to him, vertical thinking is compared to digging a hole deeper.

The problem with vertical thinking is that if you are digging the wrong hole, you will not find the solution no matter how deep you dig.

The second type of thinking is lateral or divergent thinking. Lateral thinking is compared to digging many different holes (looking for many solutions). The likelihood of finding the correct solution is substantially increased. As the Nobel laureate, Linus Pauling says, "*The best way to get a good idea is to get lots of ideas*".

Lateral thinking is essential for generating creative ideas. The three primary creativity techniques outlined in this book are designed to enhance your lateral thinking.

Studies by Marian Diamond on mice brains and other studies on human longevity found that regular good doses of thinking actually keep us healthier and make us live longer and happier lives. A group of nuns living in the mountain, all of whom were over 80 years old were found to be physically fit and mentally alert. Investigations revealed that they shared one thing in common—they loved solving puzzles! Unfortunately, less than two percent of the people think. This fact caused the famous writer, George Bernard Shaw to remark: "If I am more successful than others, and made an international reputation for myself, it is because I ***think*** (*Jig-word* 2*) as often as once a week". So, if you want to be successful, physically fit and mentally alert better, start thinking!

Stories Of Creativity

4.2 Quick Thinking Saves The Day

The Prime Minister of China entertained a presidential couple to a grand banquet. The finest crockery was used. In fact the chinaware used for the banquet included priceless national treasures from the Ming dynasty.

An aide to the Prime Minister observed that the First Lady, the wife of the visiting President was quietly slipping a priceless piece of crockery into her handbag. He reported this alarming discovery to the Prime Minister.

The problem posed a dilemma to the Prime Minister. The country could not afford to lose its priceless piece of national treasure. On the other hand, revealing the incident would be highly embarrassing and cause a diplomatic row, which must be avoided at all cost.

The Prime Minister pondered over the seemingly intractable problem for a moment and then whispered a few words to his aide closest to him.

After the dinner, the Prime Minister announced that a special entertainment program would be performed in honor of the visiting President and his wife. It was a magic show to be performed by China's best magician.

The magic show did live up to its name. It was both mystifying and highly entertaining. As a climax to the show, the magician held up a piece of chinaware similar to the one that the First Lady had taken and made it disappear with a flourish. The magician asked the Prime Minister where he would like the chinaware to reappear.

The Prime Minister thought for a moment. *"The most difficult place for it to reappear is the First Lady's handbag,"* he said.

The magician politely asked the First Lady to check her handbag and recovered the missing national treasure to the thunderous applause of the guests including the presidential couple. Thus the Prime Minister's quick thinking saved the day.

Mindxercise 4.2: Looking For Many Solutions

There are two main stumbling blocks to creativity. The first is that we tend to impose our own restrictions before even attempting to solve the problem. The second is that most of the time we look for a single right answer, instead of exploring different possibilities.

The problems below were selected to help you to overcome these two major stumbling blocks. Please refrain from taking the easy way out by referring to the answers. Remember that there is no greater joy than the joy of creativity!

1. Perfect Square : make a perfect square by moving only one match

2. Join the following dots using only one straight line

3. Making six : Add one line to make it six

4. How would you interpret the Mindbloom logo below?

MINDBLOOM

Step 3: Incubation

The mind ought to sometimes be diverted that it may return the better to thinking.

Phaedrus

If you want to develop your creativity, establish regular work habits. Allow time for the incubation of ideas, and adhere to your individual rhythm. Violations of this rhythm can retard your creative efficiency.

Eugene Raudsepp

If after intense mental efforts, no solution is forthcoming, ideas have dried up and the thinking process is unproductive then, it is time to stop. The conscious mind has done all it can for the moment. Then it is time to relax or do something else and let the subconscious mind take over. This is called incubation.

When you relax your mental defenses are down, your conscious mind becomes unburdened of the problem and your subconscious mind is set free to make new connections which are what creativity is all about. Incubating an idea is just like incubating an egg. A lot of things are happening inside which you do not see on the outside. Incubation may take minutes, hours, days, months or even years.

Incubation occurs in many ways, such as : relaxing, playing, concentrating or doing something else, daydreaming, fantasizing or even sleeping. In fact, it was found in one survey that 70 percent of inspirations leading to major scientific breakthroughs happened while the scientists were napping or sleeping! So there is some truth in the common belief that you have to sleep on your problem. Sleeping on the job may not be such a bad thing after all!

Archimedes got his inspiration in discovering the Archimedes Principle while taking his bath. Einstein solved many of his scientific problems while playing his violin or taking a nap. Robert Louis Stevenson, dreamed up complete stories to which he could return to night after night and Charles Darwin found the critical linkage in his Theory of Evolution while riding in a horse—carriage. Seymour Cray, father of the supercomputer found that digging in the tunnel under his home provided him with the best incubation.

Stories Of Creativity

4.3 The Farmer Who Had a Problem Cleaning His Teeth

Boon Su Chan, a Malaysian farmer, had difficulty removing nicotine stains from his teeth accumulated through his years of smoking. He bought and used various types of toothbrushes available in the market but none of them could do the job of removing the stubborn nicotine stains.

Boon Su left his farming and found a job in the city. However, he just could not get the problem of finding a better method of cleaning his teeth out of his mind. He paid particular attention to advertisements on toothbrushes in the hope of finding inspiration to solve the problem, but none came.

During the school holidays Boon Su decided to take his family back to his birthplace to visit his parents. While driving back, happy memories of his childhood days flooded his mind. He contrasted his experiences with those of his children who were deprived of interaction with nature.

Lost in his thoughts, he drove through the village and saw farmers hard at work at their vegetable plots. Suddenly, an inspiration flashed through his mind. He made the connection!

The farmers were using the hoe, which has a blade at right angle to the handle and is always used at a 45-degree angle. It is the most effective way to loosen the soil. The toothbrush too could be designed the same way. Using this connection, Boon Su invented the world's first swivel head vertical toothbrush, which can tilt at 45 degrees.

His Zowin toothbrush won several international awards. It provides effective cleaning even hard to reach places like the back of the teeth. Never under—estimate the power of incubation!

4.4 Movie and Car Design

Nissan Design International based in San Diego, USA was set up to design Nissan cars for the US market. It was headed by Mr. Jerry Hirshberg, the president of the company. The company was commissioned to design a new sport utility vehicle to be called the Nissan Pathfinder.

Hirshberg and his design team worked very hard for months but were unable to come out with outstanding innovative features for the new car. They were getting desperate as the deadline drew near.

Hirshberg did not panic. Instead, he took his entire staff of 50 people to the movies. The movie was Silence of the Lambs starring Jodie Foster. It was a suspense film where concentration was essential in order to follow the dialogue and the story plot. Watching the movie took the staff's minds away from the design of the car.

The brief respite from work provided a much needed incubation period for the staff. They were mentally energized after the movie and ideas began to flow. The project was successfully completed within the stipulated deadline. So next time, when you are not making any headway with your problem, take time off to incubate.

Mindxercise 4.3: Simple But Not Easy

The following problems are simple but require a creative thinking approach. They refer to real situations. To solve them, you need to get out from your conditioned frame of mind. An incubation period to hatch your solutions may be useful.

1. *Ten apples*

   At the end of a birthday party, the hostess realized that there were ten apples left in a basket. She distributed an apple to each of the ten children who were leaving. After all the ten children have taken their apples, there was still one apple left in the basket. Why?

2. *Jumping out from a 20-storey building*

   A man was drinking coffee at his table by the window. He was enjoying the view outside his window when suddenly on impulse; he jumped out of the 20-storey building. He landed safely, unhurt in any way. There was nothing to cushion his landing. How was this possible?

3. *Striking Clock*

   The clock in the clock tower of the main City Square takes 2 seconds to strike 2 o'clock. How long will it take for the clock to strike 3 o'clock?

4. *Measuring the lake*

   Suppose there is a small irregularly shaped lake behind your house. It is of variable and unknown depth. There are no rivers or streams entering or leaving the lake. How would you find the volume of water in the lake?

5. *Recorded Message*

   A man was found dead at his office desk with a pistol by his side. On the desk was a tape recorder. Pushing the play button brought the message, "*I can't take it anymore. I want to end my agony.*" Followed by the sound of a shot. The police concluded almost immediately that the man was murdered. How?

Step 4: Eureka!

A moment's insight is sometimes worth a life's experience.

Oliver Wendell Holmes

I can remember the very spot in the road, whilst in my carriage, when to my joy the solution occurred to me.

Charles Darwin

Finally, the idea hatched after the incubation period. *"Eureka"* is a Greek word that means *"I found it!"* It was made famous when Archimedes ran out naked in the street upon discovering a method to determine the purity of the gold in the King's crown (see accompanying story below). Today it denotes the feeling of exhilaration and joy when one solves a particularly difficult problem or made an important discovery.

Creativity is hard work but it is well worth the effort. As Einstein says, it is the most fundamental and beautiful experience that a person can have. It cannot be described fully in words or pictures. It can only be savored at the moment of *"Eureka!"*.

Creativity is hard work but it is well worth the effort. As Einstein says, it is the most fundamental and beautiful experience that a person can have. It cannot be described fully in words or pictures. It can only be savored at the moment of *"Eureka!"*.

Stories Of Creativity

4.5 The Naked Man Who Shouted "Eureka!" In The Street

King Heiron of Syracuse was not happy with his crown. He suspected that the goldsmith had cheated him by adding silver to the crown of pure gold that he had ordered to be made. However, he had no way to determine whether the crown was made of pure gold.

King Heiron was extremely frustrated. He paced up and down his room trying to think of a solution. Suddenly, a thought struck him. Why not ask Archimedes, the most famous scientist in the land to provide a solution? Without any hesitation, he sent for his guards to summon Archimedes to the palace.

Archimedes had no idea how it could be done as no one had ever done it before. Nevertheless, he accepted the assignment. It was not wise to make the King angry as in those days the King could easily order the execution of anyone who displeased him.

Archimedes pondered over the problem for days and nights, utilizing all his scientific skills and knowledge. But the solution still eluded him. Meanwhile, the deadline was drawing near for he had to report to the King within the next two days.

Archimedes gave up and was resigned to his fate. He talked to himself, "In two days time, I would probably present my head instead of the solution to the King." Thinking thus, he went to his favorite place for relaxation, the public Roman bath. His thoughts were no longer on the crown but on the memories of his happier days.

As he lowered himself into his favorite bathtub and watched the water level rose, an idea flashed across his mind. Archimedes was so excited by the idea that he got out of the tub immediately and ran out naked into the streets shouting, "Eureka! Eureka!" He had found the solution to the problem. Thus both Archimedes and the term "eureka" became famous.

Let's now examine Archimedes's discovery in the light of the five steps to creativity.

Step 1 : Knowledge
Archimedes had the knowledge as he was a renowned scientist.

Step 2 : Thinking
He did think long and hard over the problem.

Step 3 : Incubation
Archimedes decided to give up and went to relax in the public bath and to enjoy the memories of his happy days.

Step 4 : Eureka
The idea hatched when he watched the water rise as he lowered himself into the bathtub.

Step 5 : Development

Archimedes' solution would not have been very useful if he had gone around telling people that they could find the purity of gold by going to a public bath. Instead, he developed the idea further by utilizing his scientific background to formulate the famous Archimedes Principle which is of general application to determine the density of irregularly shaped objects.

Basically, Archimedes's creativity lies in making a connection between the displacement of water as he entered the bathtub and the density of gold. He arrived at the solution of utilizing the density of gold to determine the purity of the gold in the crown.

> Footnote:
> Archimedes confirmed the King's suspicions. The crown was not made of pure gold. The goldsmith lost his head for deceiving the King. Archimedes not only managed to keep his head intact but was rewarded with some gold as well. It pays to be creative, doesn't it?

Mindxercise 4.4: Solving Real-Life Problems

The problems below were real-life problems, which were successfully solved with ingenuity. The solutions were simple and obvious once they were known.

Try the five steps to creativity technique when trying to solve the problems. In particular, allow for an incubation period when your thoughts are jammed. Please resist the temptation to refer to the answers until you have gone through the five steps.

Don't be surprised if *you are* (*Jig-word* 3*) able to come out with your own answers which are even better than those provided in the solutions at the back of the book.

Remember that frequently the best solutions are the simplest and the most obvious, yet they are the most likely to be overlooked.

1. *The Pedestal*

    An important historical statue with a flat base was to be placed in position on a specially prepared pedestal with a flat top in a public park. The heavy marble statue was to be handled with extreme care and no part of the statue was to be damaged in any way. The statue was strapped with ropes looping over its base and lowered by means of a crane on the pedestal. The problem was how to remove the ropes from under the statue after it was correctly positioned on the pedestal. How do you do it?

2. *Shampoo and Towel*

    A social club has a problem of disappearing towels and shampoos in their bathrooms. Without checking the members bag, how would you solve the problem without causing any inconvenience to the members?

3. *Condominium and Spaciousness*

    In order to market condominiums, showrooms having the exact dimensions to be sold were built for viewing by prospective customers. These showroom were attractively furnished to entice customers. The problem was to create a perception of spaciousness for its smaller units. How would you do it?

4. *Postman and Dog*

A postman has to deliver mail to a large bungalow which was guarded by a ferocious dog. The only way to deliver the mail was for the postman to walk along a path from the gate to the front door of the house. The dog was tied to a tree and its chain was long enough for him to reach anyone walking past him. Chain fencing surrounded the house. How do you think the postman could walk safely past the dog to deliver the mail?

5. *Cable & Gorge*

Two teams of workers were sent to build a bridge across a deep, fast-flowing gorge. The main building materials consisting of cables could only be transported to one side of the gorge due to the difficult terrain on the other side. The problem was to send one end of the cables over to the team on the other side. It was too dangerous to swim across and the two teams were unable to summon for outside help. How did they finally manage to build the bridge?

Step 5: Development

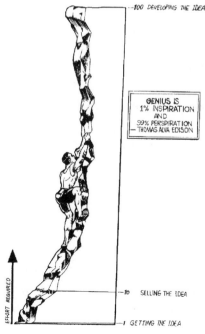

100 DEVELOPING THE IDEA

GENIUS IS
1% INSPIRATION
AND
99% PERSPIRATION
— THOMAS ALVA EDISON

EFFORT REQUIRED

10 SELLING THE IDEA

1 GETTING THE IDEA

It is difficult to say what is impossible, for the dream of yesterday is the hope of today and the reality of tomorrow.

Robert H. Goddard

Vision without action is merely a dream. Action without vision just passes the time. Vision with action can change the world!

Joel Arthur Barker

What's next after eureka? Development is about acting on an idea to make it useful, functional and if possible, profitable. On the scale (1-100) of the amount of effort required or the degree of difficulty to be overcome, getting the idea ranked as 1 and developing the idea into something tangible ranks a 100. Everyone has ideas but action in developing the idea is what differentiates the innovator from the dreamer.

In almost all cases, help from others is required. You probably have to source outside help in specific areas of expertise such as manufacturing, marketing and financing. In the case of Bette Nesmith, she had to get a chemist to help get the right formulation (quick-drying solvent and effective white pigment to cover the mistakes) and to consult a marketing expert in order to give the product a good name, Liquid Paper, and to package it attractively (small bottle with a brush).

Stories Of Creativity

4.6 The Circumcision-happy Doctor

Malaysia is an Islamic-majority country and circumcision is an essential aspect of becoming a Muslim. Dr. Gurcharan Singh had a fondness for circumcision. He did his best for his patients coming to see him but was horrified to see grotesque mutilations resulting from bad circumcision jobs that were referred to him.

Dr. Gurcharan spent years doing research on circumcision. He traveled widely, including going to Africa to personally observe how circumcision was actually carried out. All the methods involved some form of surgery and with it the inherent risks of infections, including HIV. Thus he was not satisfied. There had to be a better way, he thought.

On a particularly cold winter night during one of his overseas trips, his friend casually mentioned the subject of frostbite over dinner. Eureka! Dr. Gurcharan made the connection instantly.

Frostbite, which is caused by an external effect—the weather, could result in the body rejecting a tissue, which it can no longer support. Using the same principle, Dr. Gurcharan invented the disposable *Tara Klamp Circumcision Device.*

The device cuts off the supply of blood to the foreskin of the penis so that it can then be removed painlessly. In fact the person who has been circumcised can put on his pants immediately and carry on with his normal life.

It took Dr. Gurcharan another 20 years of painstaking development efforts before his circumcision device could be launched commercially. He filed his first patent in the U.K and thereafter to over 50 countries all over the world. Next, he spent a lot of money to get a professional designer to work out the technical details of the device. He got his doctor friends to carry out clinical trials with his prototypes. Assured of its workability, he approached a contract manufacturer to mass-produce the device.

Dr. Gurcharan went to another Design Company to come out with an attractive and effective packaging. He then appointed an exclusive distributor in Malaysia. For the export market, he set up a new company to handle exclusive distribution deals. He also had to look into marketing and promotion.

Development is undoubtedly the most difficult step in the creativity process.

Mindxercise 4.5: Developing Ideas to Practical Application

Development ensures that an idea is successfully carried through. The most difficult part of development is probably convincing others to buy your product. This is what marketing is all about. Given the idea, how would you develop a marketing campaign for the following:

1. *Trains versus Planes*
   Everyone knows that trains are much slower than planes and are less modern. However, there are two key points in the train's favor, that

is: cost and the scenic view. How would you create an advertising campaign to drive home these two points?

2. *The Potato Chips Battle*
   Pringle potato chips from Proctor and Gamble were the market leader. It was promoted as the newfangled potato chip. Upon scrutiny of its package, it was found that the list of ingredients to preserve the freshness of its chips read like a chemistry set. The label of Wise potato chips on the other hand listed the ingredients as potatoes, vegetable oil and salt. How would you do a TV commercial for Wise?

3. *Piggy-back on the Giant*
   In 1986, British Airways carried out a massive promotion in the U.S. by giving away 5200 tickets to London for flights on 10th June. A much smaller U.K airline and little known in the U.S., Virgin Atlantic Airways decided to capitalize on British Airways promotion to advertise its services. How would you have done it for Virgin Atlantic Airways?

4. *Stand out from the competition*
   At the Frankfurt International Book Fair, a small-time publisher of children's books rented a booth to promote his books. The problem was that his booth was small and insignificant among the 20 booths in his row. Another disadvantage is that his booth was situated near the middle of the row. Yet he was able to make his booth to stand out and attracted lots of children with minimum effort and expenditure. How did he do it?

5. *Creative Endorsements*
   Chupa Chups, a Spanish lollipop company intends to establish itself as the world's brand for lollipops. It already makes 4 billion lollipops a year, selling 40 flavors in 170 countries. But it is still tiny in the global market compared to such chocolate giants as Hershey Foods Corp., Mars Inc., and Nestlé. The company is using smart, creative marketing strategies to get endorsements from celebrities like Britney Spears, Madonna, Giorgio Armani, Brandy, Elton John, etc. Each one has been recorded as a Chupa Chups "celebrity sucker". How did the company do it?

RECORD YOUR
CREATIVITY BLOOM HERE

PRIMARY CREATIVITY TECHNIQUES

The basis of creativity has always been a new connection. To make connections would take hours using words. Your subconscious has to use pictures.

William J.J Gordon

Creativity And Television

There are hundreds of creativity techniques—simply hundreds! Though nearly all are good, there is the problem. That problem is having to learn and remember such a vast variety of techniques and then having to select one suitable for a specific use. It's something I'd pondered for quite some time. How to find that particular example? How to find something which, by way of analogy, I could use to show the reader just what I mean?

My definition of Creativity is *"Making the connection,"* How could I show how to do this? The task was to link multifarious "creativity techniques" to something that is simple yet could, at the same time, provide many variations. Numerous examples from single source—that was what I was after.

The answer? It took a while. Then, Eureka! I got it:. Creativity techniques and the Colour Television set. It was so obvious! The modern color TV receiver displays millions of colors, yet all of these are produced by only the *three primary spectral colors:* red, green, and blue. By sticking with this analogy, my explanation is that all creativity techniques can be classified or anchored under just three headings: Here are those **three primary creativity techniques**:

Craziness, Fantasy And Imagination

The key issue here is how to think creatively instead of thinking logically. Well, the answer is to think crazy, fantasize and to use our imagination in order to think out of the ordinary. There are many ways of doing this and I have chosen *Brainstorming* as the anchor technique. (*see Bloom 6 for details*).

Randomness

A proven way to think *out-of-the box* is to randomly select an item and associate it with your problem. Having someone who has no idea on what problem you are going to solve to make the random association for you is even better. The anchor technique is "*Making Forced Connections*" (*see Bloom 7 for details*).

Features, Characteristics And Attributes

One of the essential features of creativity is the ability to think differently from others. Therefore the key technique here is to study the features, characteristics and attributes of a product, service or process and then think of a non-conventional way of achieving better results. The anchor technique is "*Breaking Rules*" (*see Bloom 8 for details*).

Details of each of the three techniques can be found in subsequent Chapters (Blooms).

Like learning any other skill, you have to first familiarize yourself with the three primary techniques before trying to adapt, modify or combine them in different ways. Do not feel constrained by the techniques described. Once you grasp the basis and significance of the creativity techniques, you could even create your own. This is what creativity is all about.

The secret to solving problems is to find the bridge between the ways things are and the way you want them to become.

Dave Koburg

The Power Of Questions

Before you use any creativity techniques, you need to ask the right questions. Some exploratory questions, which will give you a better understanding of your problem, are the 5W's and 1H or the Five Wishes and One Hope. They are : *Who, Why, What, When, Where, and How.* It is of little use to give a brilliant solution to the wrong problem.

Suppose, your original objective is to invent a better drill. You should then ask the question: "What is it for?" The answer is : *"To make a hole"*. Once you understand this, you will not necessarily be inventing a drill but an equipment that will make holes more effectively and efficiently. Some of the equipments that can make holes include : lasers, water-jet and a hot-wire. By restricting ourselves with a statement like: *"I want to drill holes more efficiently?"* rather than *"How can I make holes more efficiently?"* we preclude our chances of coming up with other, more revolutionary methods.

Think of what you want to achieve—then ask the Five Ws and H questions. Do this first.

Do not ask questions with a narrow scope or focus. If, for example, you were in a foreign country for the first time and would like to find the best way to travel from Town A to Town B. Asking the question: *"How do I take a taxi from A to B?"*, will restrict your options. On the other hand, if you ask the question: *"How can I go from A to B?"* you will discover other means of transportation (or combination of transportation) which may be safer, cheaper, faster, more interesting and perhaps even more comfortable.

The famous scientist Albert Einstein was once asked: *"What would you do if you have 60 minutes to save the world from the collision with a large meteorite?"* Einstein replied that he would spend the first 55 minutes asking questions and the last 5 minutes to find a solution.

Restating A Problem

Re-stating the problem is also very important. For example, Rank Xerox, re-engineered itself by changing the company's mission from "The Document Processing Company" to "*The Document Company*". The changed look simple enough and only one word is dropped but that changed Rank Xerox's whole perspective and focus. It widened the scope of the company's business. And by doing so, it played a critical role in reviving Xerox's fortunes.

When Toyota Corporation of Japan asked the staff to submit: "*Ideas to Improve Productivity*", the response was rather poor. However, when the problem was re-stated as: "*How to Make Your Work Easier*". Even though both of these statements had the same end objective as far as management was concerned the way it was worded made all the difference. In. the first case, the workers' perception was that the management and owners were the beneficiaries of the project to improve productivity. In the second case, the beneficiaries were clearly the workers themselves—or this is how it was perceived.

The Ford Motor Company was in a sorry state in 1980. Then Donald E. Petersen took over as President. When Petersen took over, sales were down and Ford was losing its market share at a rapid rate.

A major factor leading to the decline was a design policy consisting of a set of strict and complicated design rules that severely hampered creativity. People weren't being encouraged to think "outside the square." The new company President replaced this rigid set of rules with a twelve-word target for the Design Centre. Here's what it said:

"*Design something that you would be proud to park in your driveway.*"

This simple directive established a winning formula. It empowered and motivated. The directive unleashed the team's creativity, thus enabling Ford's people to design the highly successful Thunderbird and Taurus of motor vehicles.

A TO Z CREATIVITY EXCITERS

The A to Z of Creativity Exciters are useful to stimulate further ideas based on the original idea or seed idea that you already have. You could select at random a few Exciters or go through the entire list if you prefer.

CREATIVITY EXCITERS

INSTRUCTIONS: Bring an idea, question or problem to this exercise as a thought that has been seeded in your mind. Review each of the words in the list below, and watch for new ideas and perspectives to come to mind in relation to your seed thought.

Adapt, alternate, analogies, action, advance it

Brainstorm, be the idea, break rules, benefits list, bigger, branch out

Challenge assumptions, combine, color it, change the problem

Draw it, doodle, deadlines, dream, deeper, delay it

Enhance, exaggerate, expand benefits, enlarge.

Features expand, fun with it, flea markets, fantasy

Group ideas, gamble, games, gather thoughts or data, germinate, gimmick

Half it, hear it, heal, hire, hunt, help, humor

Ink it, inflate it, integrate it, internalize it, I Ching, incubate it

Justify it, journal on it, juggle, join, journey

Kinky, kids' perspective, kaleidoscope, kernel

Lighten it, lengthen it, live it, let it go, listen to hunches

Magnify, minimize, modify, metaphors, mind map, merge

Nix it, negatives are . . . , name it, needs clarification, nurture

Opposites, others do it, obvious, obscure, omit, open

Picture it, perspectives change, prototype it, postpone it, persist, patterns, play

Qualify it, quicken it, question, quest, quit

Reduce, reverse, rearrange, rotate, random word, resist

Simplify, suppose, substitute, shorten, segment up to a bigger picture, sell idea

Trade shows, truncate parts, terminate, truth is . . , take a break

Un . . . , uncover, unlock, unrealistic, unite

Viewpoint change, vocalize, visualize, vacate, values, vary

Why 5 times, what if, wait, wish, withhold, witness

e**X**aggerate, x-ray it, eXtend it

Yell it, yield, yardstick, youthful

Zero base, zoom up, zoom down, zany, zigzag

Reproduced with kind permission from: Mr. John Robson

John@higherawareness.com Website: http://www.higherawareness.com

RECORD YOUR
CREATIVITY BLOOM HERE

CREATIVITY TECHNIQUE 1: BRAINSTORMING

Go ahead and be wacky. Get into a crazy frame of mind and ask what's funny about what you're doing.

Roger von Oech

By and large Brainstorming is probably the most popular, but wrongly used technique in eliciting new ideas to solve problems. It was devised and used by Alex Osborn in an advertising agency in the 1940s. Details of this ***creative*** *(Jig-word* 4)* technique were published in 1957 in a book called "Applied Imagination".

Unlike most so-called brainstorming sessions where a group of people sits around a table to get some ideas, real brainstorming is more structured with specific guidelines to follow. It is designed to get a continuous and free-flow of ideas without any inhibition whatsoever.

Brainstorming is about getting as many ideas as possible from a group of people in a short time.

Fantasy And Imagination

There are many variations to the brainstorming technique devised by Alex Osborn. One of them is *"Displayed Thinking"* used by the Walt Disney Corporation. One wall of a room is allocated for the team to display their ideas in the form of words, sketches or diagrams. Any member of the team is free to display his/her ideas on this wall. In this way, ideas just grow and grow. There is tremendous mental stimulation.

A second way is to have a facilitator immediately record ideas in writing on a whiteboard or butchers paper. The group call out their ideas; the facilitator jots them down. This is probably the most commonly used in the business world today. With a good facilitator, the ideas come thick and fast.

Disadvantage to this second method: Often an idea, thrown up in a terse sentence is subject to misinterpretation, so the facilitator might ask for approval of the group as he paraphrases or abbreviates. This is why a picture or diagram is usually better. It is a truism that "one picture is worth a thousand words."

Another variation on brainstorms is called *"Brain-Writing"*. This technique is valuable for people who were not so expressive with their ideas and who may prefer anonymity to voicing out their ideas directly. Here, slips of papers are passed around for members to add to or combine ideas on the list. The sessions are less dynamic than brainstorming. This method may be more acceptable in a conservative setting. It certainly isn't the most effective, in my opinion.

> *The best way to get a good idea is to get a lot of ideas.*
> Linus Pauling

Fantasy and imagination complement brainstorming. They are powerful tools to enhance the effectiveness and productivity. Children are naturally gifted in this. Adults, too, can re-discover this skill by watching fantasy movies and reading fairy tales. In fact, many famous personalities retained this ability through their adulthood. They include scientists like Albert Einstein and Nikolai Tesla, philosophers and mathematicians like Rene Descartes, musicians such as Beethoven, artists like Michelangelo, writers like Robert Louis Stevenson, cartoonists like Stan Lee (Marvel comics : X-men, Spiderman, etc.) and movie-makers like Steven Spielberg (of Star Wars fame). The principle is simple—words have limitations; fantasy and imagination have none.

Guidelines For Brainstorming

There are four basic guidelines to follow in brainstorming.

1. *No criticism*
    Criticism of any idea expressed is absolutely forbidden.

2. *No evaluation*
    There should not be any evaluation of ideas during the idea generation stage. Participants are encouraged to say whatever comes into their mind without self-censorship. In fact the slogan is "The crazier, the better".

3. *Quantity of ideas*
    The very essence of brainstorming is to get as many ideas as possible. Quantity is more important than quality. The evaluating, quantifying, and decision-making comes much later.

4. *Cross-fertilize* (This is usually done as ideas begin dwindle out)
    Participants are encouraged to combine or modify any of the ideas expressed to enable the generation of even more new ideas. There should not be any individual ownership of any specific ideas. Group ownership is important. It will discourage egotistical comparisons.

    In addition, the following procedures will also help in facilitating a successful brainstorming session.
    *   There should be no outside observers. Also, no audio or visual recording devices. This is important. Participants should feel comfortable in suggesting crazy ideas which, if made known to

non-participants, may make them feel foolish. And certainly no notes of 'who made what' suggestions should be kept.

- All ideas should be numbered for easy reference and displayed for all participants to see. This helps with cross-referencing when the 'combining—modifications' stage is reached.

- If necessary, the list of ideas generated is to be distributed to participants at the end of the session. This will allow them plenty of time to put an "incubation phase" into the procedure. All those ideas are almost certain to generate even further ideas when submitted to the group's subconscious' processes.

- There should be a facilitator to conduct the session and someone to list down the ideas. This can sometimes be done by the same person if the brainstorming group is small, e.g. half-a-dozen or less. However, in a larger, more dynamic group, it might be necessary to have a separate person—or even two persons and two whiteboards—to get down all those fast-flowing ideas.

During brainstorming, participants are expected to use their right brain (creative thinking) rather than logical left brain thinking. A good brainstorming session occurs when there are more crazy ideas than logical ones. Generally, crazy ideas by themselves are not useful. They are meant to *trigger* innovative ideas, which are ultimately practical. Also, crazy ideas are often highly amusing. With people laughing and happy, the creativity often steps up a gear.

Stages Of Brainstorming

1. *Warming up*
    This loosens up participants, engendering a light-hearted, happy state of mind. Generally, five to ten minutes would be sufficient. The topic selected in the warming up exercise needn't have any connection with the actual problem. It's probably better if it doesn't. What's chosen should be one that will bring out lots of laughter and fun for participants, for example: "List all the uses for underwear." Nylon panty-hose was a good substitute for a broken fan belt for a 1948 Bedford truck, according to the writers of the Brian Dehenehu film, "The Lion of Africa."
    Then we get into the real game.

2. *Restate the problem* (Step 1 of Creativity Process)
   The participants are asked to restate the problem in different ways. Frequently, asking the right question puts the team halfway to coming out with a solution.

3. *Brainstorming* (Step 2 of Creativity Process)
   This is the *actual* brainstorming session as described above. A time frame should be decided in advance. In all probability, the bigger the group the longer the time. Typically it would range from somewhere between 10 and 30 minutes.

4. *Incubation* (Step 3 of Creativity Process)
   This is the break period between the idea-generation stage and the evaluation stage. It could just be a short coffee break. Then, it could be a much longer break: half-a-day, several days or even weeks, depending on the complexity of the problem. Usually, if it's longer than that coffee break, the list of recorded ideas is distributed to participants for them to mull through. During this period we're giving the subconscious minds' of our participants a chance to come up with answers. It might be advisable to tell participants that if they do come up with answers, to jot them down. They can then be presented at the next stage . . .

5. *Evaluation Stage* (Step 4 of Creativity Process)
   This is where connections of ideas are made to produce useful and practical ideas. It is equivalent to the *"Eureka"* stage of the creativity process. Some ideas could be discarded here. Others amalgamated. The thinning out period continues until a consensus is reached as to the best solution. For example: the earlier idea to send the boss to the moon on a bicycle would probably get the chop here. We're getting very serious at this stage. The solution or solutions are now being defined. We have our answer or answers.

6. *Implementation Plan & Strategy* (Step 5 of Creativity Process)
   Once the possible solutions are identified, it's time to come out with a proper plan and strategy for implementation. Creativity still rules. But it's directed towards how to *successfully implement* that new and brilliant idea which came out of the main brainstorming session.

Stories Of Creativity

6.1 The Seeing Shoes With Cow's eyeballs

A shoe manufacturing company carried out a brainstorming exercise to get ideas to develop a new line of shoes. Initially, the problem was stated as the type of shoes to be introduced. Were they ladies fashion shoes, men's leather shoes, sports shoes, etc.? After considering many different statements to the problem, it was decided that they should concentrate on jogging shoes with unique features.

Many ideas were thrown about; some suggested putting coiled springs in the soles, detachable and changeable parts, using pastel colors and so on. However, the most ridiculous and craziest idea came from a salesman who lived near an abattoir. His suggestion seemed to be absolutely crazy!

Why not sew cow's eyes on them?" The salesman knew these would be readily available from the nearby abattoir. *"Sew them to the front of the shoes. Let the shoes see where they are going?"*

Everyone had a good laugh and agreed that this was the craziest idea in the brainstorming session. Crazy is crazy. The manager of the company, who was the facilitator for the session, asked the participants to focus on this idea before announcing a tea break. *"Cow's eyes . . . eyes . . . Think 'eyes'."*

It was evaluation time after the tea break. This was the time when the practical aspects of the idea had to be considered. A translation of the idea into practical form included installing optical lenses instead of cow's eyes; having a built-in shock absorber in front to absorb the impact of kicking something hard; sewing on artificial eyes to give the shoes a unique identity, and so on.

In the midst of the discussion, someone suggested that instead of the shoes being able to see where they were going, it would be far better for *other people* to see where the shoes were going. A shoe designer at the meeting immediately made a connection. Yes! Shoes with a *reflector*! Like the reflector used in motor vehicles. This man suggested adding a reflective strip to the heel of the shoe. It could be seen from behind. The idea was taken up for development.

Today we see jogging shoes with luminous strips, which glow in the dark so that the jogger can be spotted. But it goes much further than that. This invention spawned a whole new industry dealing with luminous strips. We see them now on tracksuits, helmets and bicycle pedals, the list goes on . . .

So, you see, one never knows what new business opportunities may arise as a result of a crazy idea!

6.2 The Paint That Exploded Off The Walls

A paint factory held a brainstorming session to get innovative ideas. How could they sell more paint? Upon examining the problem, it was found that the main market was in *repainting* rather than painting new buildings for the first time. This was because, at the time, few new buildings were being constructed. Thus the question that was chosen for brainstorming was "How to encourage house-owners to repaint their houses?"

Many ideas were suggested including: special promotions, free overseas trips linked to painting competitions. However, the craziest idea came from the accounts clerk. He suggested that gunpowder be mixed with the paint, so that instead of the tedious process of scraping the paint off the wall, all that was needed to light it up to cause an explosion. This would blow the paint right off the walls! Crazy? You'd think so.

The factory manager didn't dismiss it.

Instead, he gave it considerable consideration. Accordingly, an incubation period of one week was set to allow for the germination of a practical application to the idea.

The company's quality control chemist made a connection. Why not use chemical solvents? With her knowledge of chemistry, she was able to offer a practical solution. Maybe blowing the paint off wasn't exactly right but . . .

The final solution was to use a combination of two solvents. The first solvent was mixed into the can of paint itself. The second solvent would be brushed over the layer of paint the house-holder wanted to remove. Done right, *the chemical reaction between the two solvents would be such that it caused the whole layer of paint to be easily peeled off the wall.*

An intensive research was carried out to find the best combination of solvents. Finally the new product was successfully introduced to the market as "specialty paint." It proved a great success.

Another victory for brainstorming!

6.3 The Business Of Setting Fire To Competitors' Shops

A family-run mixed—business was doing really badly due to the competition from supermarkets. The shop-owner, who had previously attended a brainstorming seminar, decided to brainstorm in an effort to discover new ways to improve his business. How could he beat the big companies?

The shop-owner, his wife and two sons explored the dimension of the problem. They had to focus on how to better the competition from other mixed business-sundry-type shops *as well* as from the supermarkets. It didn't look as though it'd be easy.

The owner's wife suggested concentrating on a smaller range of goods with high profit margins. The man liked the idea. Then it was proposed that they sell only food products. One of the sons picked up on the idea and suggested cooked food. The other son related cooking to fire, and suggested the crazy idea of setting fires to all the competitors' shop in the vicinity!

The shop-owner made an immediate connection between this crazy idea and the insurance agent who had come to see him earlier. Eureka! He'd got it. No, they wouldn't burn down their competitors' premises—*they* go into the fire insurance business. This they did, and they prospered. They prospered because of this decision as there was hardly any competition in the fire insurance business at that time.

So it's very beneficial to have illogical or crazy thinking before logical evaluation.

Mindxercise 6: Have Fun With Brainstorming

Brainstorming sessions should always be conducted in an atmosphere of fun and laughter. In such an atmosphere, mental inhibitions break down and large numbers of ideas are generated. The exercise below gives you the opportunity to have fun.

Problems have been successfully solved through brainstorming. If you have difficulty convincing others to join you, you could try solo brainstorming. You could scribble or doodle away on pieces of paper. Have fun!

1. A company which exports vases has problems with its workers who wrap up the vases with old newspapers. The workers like to read the papers thereby affecting their productivity. Assuming that *you are* (*Jig-word* 5) the owner, what would you do to put a stop to this?
2. A biscuit factory has plenty of leftover biscuit crumbs. Could you help the owner find new uses for the crumbs so that they become a new and profitable product for the company?

3. A telephone company wants to reward its loyal customers with a unique gift that will remind them of the telephone. Try to brainstorm to get innovative ideas.

4. A food seasoning company is holding a brainstorming session to find ways to boost sales in a saturated market. Could you help out?

5. The shop to your left is doing a brisk business during the year-end sale. The shop to your right is likewise doing good business with its summer fashion sale. Your shop is in between these two shops. Brainstorm on how you could improve your sales too.

RECORD YOUR
CREATIVITY BLOOM HERE

CREATIVITY TECHNIQUE 2: FORCING NEW CONNECTIONS

Some men see things as they are and ask why. I dream of things that never were and ask, why not?

Robert F. Kennedy

Forcing New Connections

Making connections where none existed before is what creativity is all about. Therefore *forcing* new connections is a very useful technique to enhance our creativity. The essence of this technique is about *randomness*. Force a connection of your problem with something selected at random. There are practically *unlimited* possible connections that can be made.

There are several ways to do this:

1. Observation

This is the most effective tool for making forced connections. Observation simply means look around you—and try to make *connections* between things. These things may show a similarity or may be totally unrelated.

Akio Maita, a sales and marketing executive at the Bandai Company in Japan, through her observations created "Tamagotchi," a virtual pet. Tamagotchi became a worldwide craze. Akio Maita had observed that young Japanese liked to flash their portable hand-phones and pocket pagers in the streets of Tokyo. Meanwhile, other Japanese were keeping tiny pets in their cramped apartments. Mobile phones and pets . . .

Akio made a forced connection between the two phenomena. She developed the concept of a "portable digital pet." It was an egg-shaped key-chain-type device with three buttons. One button to feed and to give medication, another to bathe, and a third to clean up the droppings of the virtual-chicken portrayed in the gadget.

The name Tamagotchi was coined from the Japanese words for egg and watch.

2. Random Word

In this technique, try to relate your problem to a randomly chosen word. The word can be chosen by pointing your finger at a word in the randomly open page of a dictionary, book, magazine or a newspaper. The element of chance is increased if you keep your eyes shut.

A Japanese bread producer made a random connection between bread and the word *"can"* and came out with a successful new product—canned bread! However, random connections, especially when used with words, are seldom that simple. Direct connections are usually rare. Most of the time you have to go through a whole series of connections before hitting on the right one.

Suppose you want to design a new kitchen knife and found the word "clock" by pointing at a word at random in a magazine. From "clock" you can make a whole series of associations like : time, round, battery, winding mechanism, fast, slow, late, punctual, digital, analogue, round, square, black, green, hands, etc. If any of the words trigger a practical connection, you may stop. If not, you have to carry on, or just select one of the word associations that you prefer.

Let's say you prefer the word "hands". Now focus on the characteristic of the hand. The hand can be used for holding things; wear rings on the fingers; play music; shake hands with another; deliver a punch, etc. There is a connection between the knife and the hand holding things. In cutting, you need one hand to hold the knife and another to hold the thing we want to cut. If you are not careful, you may cut your hand! Can we protect your hand from the knife?

Well, you can. You can wear a glove that is hard enough to prevent the penetration of the knife. If it is hard, could you make it flexible enough to bend your fingers and be able to grasp the object that you are cutting? After thinking this through, the solution is to have a steel glove made in the form of flexible netting. This product is actually available. It deviates from the original intention of "designing a special knife."

To be creative, you have to take advantage of the unexpected.

3. Quotations & Proverbs

In this case, try to associate your problem with a randomly selected quotation. It could be taken from a book of quotations, a volume of poetry, a holy script, or the complete works of William Shakespeare—anywhere, really.

Now, suppose you have a problem. In this instance it's of heavy school bags which young children have to carry to school every day. You're worried about their long-term health. You find you've selected the lines: *"A mechanical instrument of torture"* from the poem—*Creativity Explosion* from this book.

What does torture remind you of? Ghastly things that cause pain and suffering to the victim? Yes. There are two things you can do. The first is to *prevent* the torture from taking place. The second is to *relieve the effect* of the torture. One way to prevent torture is to lock up all the instruments of torture so that others can't get access to it. This "lock it away" thought triggers the connection to lock up the school bags in the school. Here, the solution is to leave the schoolbags at the school. Homework can be done in the school itself. Students only bring back the actual books that they want to read, or the written exercises they want to revise, instead of the whole lot.

4. Food

Many consumer products have been created by using the power of connection with food. For example, in the 1920s, the giant multinational consumer products company, Proctor & Gamble, wanted to create a new soap. They wanted something radically different.

Vic Mills, a chemical engineer with Proctor & Gamble, made a connection between soap and ice-cream. He wondered what would happen if he put liquid soap through an ice-cream machine. It probably occurred to him that the machine would add some air into the soap mixture as it hardened into a bar. It did. The result was the world's first *floating soap*! It was an instant hit. Children loved it. So besides being a great commercial success, the air-filled "Ivory Soap" as it was called, made it into the "Soap Makers Hall of Fame."

These are only four of the countless of ways in which you can make a forced connection. You can, of course, create your own techniques for making connections. Use whichever technique you are comfortable with. There is no one best way. It's just a matter of preference. However, always remember to return to the fundamentals of creativity (the Five Steps) when you are stuck. An incubation period is almost always useful.

> *How many ideas hover dispersed in my head of which Many a pair if they should come together, could bring about the greatest of discoveries.*
>
> Georg Christopher Lichtenberg

STORIES OF CREATIVITY

7.1 The Students Who Shouted "Fire!"

You've no doubt heard the story of "*The Boy Who Cried, Wolf!*" At the third cry, nobody came to help the boy as they thought he was, once again, playing a prank. Unfortunately, the Fire Brigade is obliged to *always* respond. They have to, so the local Fire Brigade station had a serious problem. It had been receiving many crank calls reporting false fires. This, of course jeopardized the fire-fighters work in responding to real fires. Investigation revealed that most of the calls came from bored teenage students who wanted to have some fun. How could the Fire Fighting authorities deal with this problem?

Talks given by Fire Brigade officials to schools and warnings of strong disciplinary action did not bring about the desired effect. The hoax calls continued.

The Fire Chief decided to use the "random word association" technique to find a solution. He closed his eyes and opened the pages of the magazine he was reading. He let chance guide his finger to a particular word. When he opened his eyes he found that the word was "invite".

The Fire Chief then called a meeting of a few of his senior officials to make a forced connection between the problem of crank calls and the word "invite".

Many connections were suggested. One suggestion was to invite the Minister of Education to issue an appeal to stop the crank calls over TV and radio. Another suggestion was to invite residents in the area to an exhibition on fire prevention. However, the suggestion, which captured the interest of the Fire Chief, *was to invite teenage students in the area* to visit the Fire Brigade Station and to help man the 911 fire-emergency telephone lines.

This proposal was accepted and implemented.

The results were dramatic. Crank calls dropped to an almost negligible level. Later it was found that first-hand knowledge of the dangers of false alarm calls turned the student volunteers, who manned the 911 lines into crusaders who convinced their fellow students not to make any more crank calls. And a moral here: In the carrot and stick method of persuasion, the carrot is always superior. Threatening rarely helps. Encouragement works wonders.

7.2 VIP Day For Taxi Drivers

The communications director of a large corporation was chairing a meeting to garner ideas. The company would shortly be opening a new shopping complex and they wanted to make the opening ceremony a big event. The director decided to use the 'Forced Connection Technique' to gather ideas from his team.

The meeting spent a few minutes determining the type of forced connections to be made. Someone suggested that since color would be an important aspect of the décor, it should be used for forcing connections. This was readily agreed upon, and through random selection, the color yellow was chosen.

All sorts of objects with the color yellow were brought up. They included flowers, fruits, clothing, buildings and several other ideas. While the discussion was going on, the director took a glance out of the window. A row of yellow-top taxis lining up in front of the hotel across the road caught his eye. Why not anchor the connection to those taxis? Taxi drivers are very influential in spreading the word.

Also, since taxis played an important role in bringing shoppers, the cosmetic counter girl suggested that taxi drivers be invited to the opening. Seizing on the idea, the marketing executive proposed that ***if*** (*Jig-word* 6) taxi drivers were invited as VIP guests to officiate at the opening, it would do away with the cumbersome protocol of associated with a prominent personality, a lot of irrelevant political speeches and the like, and would probably reduce costs as well.

Despite apprehensions raised by others at the meeting, this chairman liked the idea. He decided to explore it further. Finally, it was decided that there would be no other guests except the taxi drivers of the city. They would be given VIP treatment. They be provided with a special certificate, discount coupons, and gifts. They'd be made to feel really special.

The event was a success that attracted intense media attention because of its uniqueness. The new shopping complex did a booming business—taxi drivers recommended it as the first choice for their clients. There couldn't be a better advertisement.

7.3 The Magic Tablet Promotion

New ideas were required for the launch of a health food product. This product was to be targeted at professionals. The goal was maximum credibility and endorsement by professionals would provide this. The marketing manager came very early to work, hoping that the quietness of the morning would provide a conducive atmosphere for him to make a forced connection. The forced connection would be between the concepts of product and the professionals to be targeted.

Sitting down by his desk, he jotted down a list of the various professions engineering, teaching, research, science and so on. The last profession on the list, was doctors. This was because the marketing manager felt that the doctors would be the most difficult people to market to.

Having decided on the doctors as the least likely customers, the manager proceeded to make a forced connection. He sketched out all the possible items associated with being a medical man: syringe, stethoscope, thermometer, medicines, etc. He tried to relate each one of these with the product, but just could not come out with any feasible connections. Nothing seemed to work.

The morning was getting brighter. Soon his colleagues would be coming to work. This wasn't so good. The manager glanced at his watch and remembered that it was time for his fizzy vitamin C drink. He took out the effervescent vitamin C tablet and dropped it into a glass of water, watching the thousands of tiny bubbles rising to the top.

Eureka! He'd got it!

In the marketing campaign, an attractively packaged tablet would be attached to each product. That was the way. All that the buyer needed to do was to drop the effervescent tablet into a glass of water and watch as the tablet dissolved in a burst of bubbles. When the tablet had dissolved sufficiently, a plastic slip would float to the surface. The slip would indicate the type of gift that the buyer had won.

This novelty of the promotion excited the public to the extent that it even elicited coverage by the press. Needless to say, it was a great success. Sales of the newly launched health food were beyond expectation.

Mindxercise 7: Making Your Own Connections

We are making connections all the time as part of the learning process. For instance, we refer to the bulls and the bears in the stock market, cash cows for a profitable product line, sudden death in sports and so on. Try to make your own connections in solving the problems below:

1. A children's ward of a hospital provided teddy bears to keep its young patients entertained. The teddy bears were so popular that some children took them home when they were discharged from the hospital. How would you solve this problem without causing inconvenience to the hospital staff or the children?

2. Mr. Earl Dickson had a wife who often cut or burnt herself in the kitchen. Each time, he had to cut a piece of gauze and tape to bandage gauze. In time he became an expert at bandaging.

Finally, he devised a special bandage, which his wife could apply it by herself. What do you think he came out with?

3. Levi Strauss, the original jeans maker came out with the latest concept for jeans by making a connection between jeans and engineering. Can you guess what it is and what do you think are the unique features of the jeans?

4. Samuel Morse, the inventor of the telegraph, was looking for a way to keep his telegraph signals flowing strong over great distances. No matter how hard he tried, the signal would fade in proportion to the distance traveled. One day, while he was travelling on a stagecoach he noticed that the Stagecoach Company periodically harnessed new teams of horses to keep the coaches to run on schedule. Making the connection, Morse created a system that is used even today to keep telecommunication signals strong. Could you guess what it was?

5. A Swiss amateur-mountaineer George de Mestral took his dog for a nature hike. They returned home covered with burrs, a type of thorn—like seed-sacs that cling to animal fur in order to travel to fertile new planting grounds. With a burning curiosity, he examined the burrs under the microscope. The burrs consisted of small hooks that enabled them to cling tightly to the tiny loops in the fabric of his pants. He made a connection and invented a very useful fastening material. What invention did George make?

6. Two radio announcers were having a bet on the radio show. Whoever has less calls will have to walk naked down the busiest street in the midst of shopping centres right in the heart of the city. The woman lost. How did she keep her promise, yet maintaining her modesty, bearing in mind also that is was illegal to walk naked in public?

RECORD YOUR
CREATIVITY BLOOM HERE

CREATIVITY TECHNIQUE 3: BREAKING THE RULES

Hell, there are no rules here—we're trying to accomplish something.

Thomas Edison

Creativity is includes discovering, experimenting, inventing, growing, taking risks, breaking rules, making mistakes and having fun.

Mary Lou Cook

Challenge the rules and try to break them. Just because things have always been done in a certain way does not mean that there are no better ways of doing them. In fact, many true and successful entrepreneurs have prospered by doing things differently. Creative thinkers get their original ideas when they challenge and reverse the obvious. In fact the greatest obstacle to creativity is when **you think you are not creative** (*Jig-word* 7).

Apple Computer founders, Steve Jobs and Steve Wozniak revolutionized the computer industry when they reverse almost everything that IBM did and almost destroyed the computer giant. As a result of their efforts, computers became affordable to the public.

Dr. Edward Jenner discovered smallpox vaccine when he studied the dairymaids who did not get infected with smallpox rather than examining people who had the disease.

Henry Ford invented the assembly line when he challenged the assumption that people have to move to their place of work. Instead he introduced the system of conveyor belts which brought work to the people. Thus began the era of mass production.

Many parents complained about their children being addicted to computer games without hardly any physical activity. Nintendo broke the rules of the computer games by introducing Wii. Wii started the motion-control revolution by enabling players to actually have exercise while playing the games. Furthermore, instead of shooting at villains, Wii motion controllers enable them to measure their fitness levels and sporting skills. Microsoft Kinect Xbox 360 went one step ahead and did away with the motion controller altogether.

Another man who reversed the way of looking at a problem was Dr. Edward Jenner. Why was it that dairymaids hardly ever contracted small pox? Instead of examining and trying to determine why people *got* the disease, he took a different approach: why didn't they get it?

Henry Ford invented the assembly line when he challenged a common assumption. That assumption was that people have to move around their place of work. Theyhad to move from one pile of materials to another, one machine to another. They had to go their place of work. There was always a requirement to walk about. Instead, Ford introduced the system of conveyor belts which brought work to the people. Thus began the era of mass production which changed the world.

There was also a legend of how Alexander the Great became the conqueror of nearly half of the known world by breaking the rules. When young Alexander at the age of 23 arrived at the city of Gordium, he was told about the prophecy of the Gordian Knot. On a marble slab were engraved these words *"Whosoever can untie this knot can conquer the world"*. For over a 100 years, many had tried but no one could untie the complex knot with their fingers as the ends were tucked in, well concealed and untraceable. After trying in vain to untie the knot with his hands, Alexander raised his sword and slashed the knot into half, thereby untying the knot by breaking the rules and making the prophecy come true.

The story of the Gordium knot raises a very important point. Anyone could have easily untied the knot with a sharp instrument like Alexander did, yet none did so. This was because they were stymied by their self—imposed rule of using their fingers. This was never mentioned as a condition.

Let's ponder over this for a moment. Our self-imposed rules such as *"it has usually been done this way"* or *"this has never been tried before"* frequently prevents us from solving a problem. Are you guilty of this?

Breaking Rules Deliberately

Alexander the Great

So the young Macedonian conqueror broke the rules deliberately. Breaking rules can be done deliberately—or it can be done accidentally. Both knowledge and ignorance can be harnessed to create practical, creative ideas. Knowledge can solve problems. But sometimes ignorance is needed to point us towards the right path.

Firstly let's examine the technique of breaking rules deliberately. To do this, you need to understand the rules. First, you would need to list down as many characteristics, features or attributes of a product, service or a system as possible. Then you'd examine each of them, and think of different approaches for each one. This is a systematic way.

For example, in a normal zoo, the animals are in cages or some kind of enclosures to prevent them from escaping. We don't want the tigers wandering into the zoo's coffee shop. Also, most zoos are only opened during the day-time. Pity, for this is the time nocturnal animals are resting or sleeping in their dens or behind the bushes. The Singapore Zoo does the opposite. It has a: "*Night Safari Zoo*" where the animals roam freely during the hours of darkness—and the visitors are cloistered in a motor vehicles for their safety. Not bad, eh? But don't run out of petrol . . .

Breaking Rules Unknowingly

Now we come to the second way—breaking rules unknowingly.

Studies have shown that prior knowledge could pose the greatest obstacle to creative thinking. This holds true particularly for professionals who have a strong theoretical foundation. As a result, such professionals have a very structured way of looking at a technical problem. In such a case, get someone who is not in the field of expertise to stimulate new approaches by breaking rules unknowingly. People who did not know that things have never been done before, frequently made breakthroughs! (Please refer to *Bloom 1—You Do Not Need To Be An Expert To Create Breakthroughs*).

A hotel was planning renovations. It wanted to upgrade its hotel facilities. One particular planned renovation was to add a new lift (elevator) to the building. A group of professionals including engineers, architects and lift experts surveyed the ground floor to find the most suitable spot to cut a hole through the ceiling to install the lift. They couldn't find such a spot; the ceiling housed gas pipes, electrical conduits, water pipes and sewage connections. It seemed just about hopeless.

It so happened that a janitor, cleaning the floor nearby, overhead the professionals discussing where they would drill the holes for the lift. The more the professionals suggested various ways to inspect the ceiling above, the more angry the janitor became. Eventually, he could contain himself no longer:

"It's easy for you guys to drill holes. But I'm the one expected to clean up all the mess! Why don't you build your lift outside and let the passengers have a good view as well!"

The architect, engineers, and elevator experts weren't amused. In fact they felt downright insulted. But somebody in management took notice. Finally, it dawned on them that it was an excellent and feasible solution to their problem.

Today we have marvelous glass-bubble lifts outside buildings that people love. Such views! And it happened because a janitor, ignorant of the problems of lift and elevator construction, came up with an idea.

"Ignorant" people can become the best rule breakers! Do invite non—experts to attend your meetings. You will not be wasting your time.

Children, too, are excellent sources to provoke *"out-of-the-box"* thinking. Dr. Edwin Land invented the Polaroid instant camera after his young daughter innocently remarked that photos should be made available immediately after being taken. Do involve children in your problem-solving or idea generation sessions. They are the best creativity stimulant that you can find! They haven't learned yet what cannot be done.

STORIES OF CREATIVITY

8.1 The Apple Which Almost Destroyed IBM

IBM is still one of the largest and most formidable computer companies in the world. But back in the 1970s it was the largest by far. It practically monopolized the computer business. When people said the word, "Computer" the next word that sprang to mind was "IBM."

IBM's success was attributed to what was, at that time, a set of rules which governed its business. Everything was strictly, and I mean, strictly, quality—controlled to the extent that management was just about paranoid. How best to ensure this high quality? How? By controlling everything from the raw material stage to the end product ready for sale. IBM manufactured its own microprocessors, which formed the heart of their computers. They did their own software. Couldn't trust others with this so essential operation. Then there were their highly trained and technically savvy sales people. It was a complete enclave rebuking any outside interference . . . or advice.

To top all this off, IBM had a strict policy of sealing its computers' covers. Only authorized personnel could open them. IBM didn't want rival companies stealing their ideas. If an unauthorized person did open up an IBM computer, the computer's warranty would be invalidated. This, the great company thought, would ensure they always maintained their dominant market position. How wrong they were.

As mentioned earlier in this book, along came two your genius's, Steven Jobs and Stephen Wozniak. The two were college dropouts. Could anyone take them seriously? The pair set to work building their own computers. They didn't have a lot of money. They did have a dream.

How could they make a computer? It had to be small. They didn't have the resources of the big guys. They started their tiny company. They called it Apple.

Apple had no resources to manufacture its own microprocessors, so these young men were obliged to buy them from other manufacturers. They had no money to hire software experts. They got around this by subcontracting this side of the business out to another upstart firm: Microsoft. And being such a small show, Apple, had hardly any sales personnel. Unlike IBM, that had all the contacts and a lot of contracts, the lads from Apple went straight to the public. They make their machines and sell them direct from retail stores.

This was a big gamble. Sales people in retail stores, at that time, had virtually no knowledge about computers. These little boxes with keyboards and cathode-ray tube screens, what were they? But word was getting round. Just like with amateur radio operators, there were lots of people out there only too willing to dabble with something new. And one thing that really attracted such enthusiasts was the fact that they could open up those boxes, look inside, do some figuring. They could tinker and add.

The same enthusiasts started to talk with one another, publish magazines on computers. There were articles on circuit boards, microchips, even whisperings of a *"World Wide Web"* open to all. These were the sorts of things that IBM had been hoping to avoid. You see, Apple was designed to be opened by users who were free to add or modify its circuit boards. For the PC technical enthusiast, this was the Holy Grail.

By their innovative approach, which broke almost all the rules that had made IBM successful, Steve Jobs and Stephen Wozniak revolutionized and transformed the computer industry. They broke another rule. They made the personal computer affordable to the public. Unlike IBM, which had been catering only to business users, Apple made the PC affordable to nearly everyone.

For a while though, even Apple's fortunes began to decline. They were too much into the business side of things and not enough into innovation and creativity. It took the return of Steve Jobs as the CEO to revitalise the company's fortunes. His return signalled the revival of creativity and breaking rules. What were some of these rules that were broken? Well, the standard, grey computer was suddenly produced in a multitude of colours.

There were translucent PCs and attractive iBook notebooks, computers that come with a handle.

Steve broke the rules on the selling of songs by the album (audios CDs or tapes) where you have to buy the entire album even though all you want is one song. He did this by introducing *iTunes*, where you can *"buy one song at a time"* by downloading from the internet. He also created iPods which can hold thousands of songs in a portable casing, smaller than a cigarette box! This in turn led to the development of podcasts, where anyone can broadcast songs or other information through the Internet without owning a studio.

Apple's introduction of the *iPhone* dethroned Nokia's No.1 mobile phone position as the market leader. This was soon followed by the computer tablet, the *iPad*, a revolutionary touch-screen computer with close to a million applications. Indeed Apple has been voted as the most innovative company in the world!

See what I mean about not being bound by rules? Let's take a look at another example . . .

8.2 Michael Dell Broke The Rules On Computer Innovations

When Michael Dell was a freshman at the University of Texas, he had a dream of beating the computer giant IBM in the computer business. What an audacious dream for a 19 year-old! No one believed him.

Dell created PCs Limited in 1984, using his university dormitory room to assemble computers from stock components. A year later, he dropped out of his university to focus on his business.

The company changed its name to *"Dell Computer Corporation"* in 1988 and began expanding globally.

Dell changed the meaning of *"innovation"* as it relates to the high-tech computer business. Before him, innovation referred to the research by engineers working in pricey research and development labs inventing high-margin products and technologies. His innovation was in distributing and selling computers direct to the customers, bypassing the dealers. The second rule he broke was to pioneer in the "configure to order" approach to manufacturing, delivering individual PCs configured to customer specifications.

However, Dell's greatest achievement was pioneering, and perfecting the art of e-commerce. In 1994, his company became the first PC maker to have a web presence. Dell had turned his company's website into an engine for mass customization—a brilliant extension to his direct-sales approach. By 1999, Dell was the largest seller on the Internet, trouncing Amazon. com eBay, and Yahoo! combined.

Breaking rules made Dell the largest PC company in the world, even overtaking Compaq. And it didn't stop there. Compaq was forced to merge with Hewlett Packard just to ensure its continued survival.

8.3 The Restaurant That Changes Price While You Are Eating

A restaurant located at a major stock exchange wanted to portray a distinctive identity. We'll call the owner, Harriet. Harriet achieved this by breaking the rules the majority of restaurants follow. Harriet decided to list the usual features of an up-market restaurant, the usual rules, and the corresponding ways to break these rules.

Features	Usual Rules	Breaking Rules
Price	Fixed	Variable
Menu	Standard	Different
Orders	Taken by Head Waiter	No Head Waiter
Ambience	Relaxed	Chaotic
Service	Tips	No Tips

From the beginning Harriet was committed to breaking the rules. This was her way to create a *distinctive* identity. She didn't desire to be like the others—she wanted to attract new business.

After thinking over the problem for a whole day without making any headway, this Harriet went to see a movie in order to relax her mind. The film was about a girl who, as an undercover agent, frequently changed her appearance to get the desired information. One moment she could be wearing a cheap tee-shirt with worn-out jeans and in the next scene she would be wearing a gorgeous and expensive evening gown. The heroine was a chameleon, changing constantly to suit the background.

In the midst of this film, an idea suddenly struck the restaurant Harriet. She made a connection between changing clothes, the stock exchange and price!

Harriet went on to create a highly popular and successful restaurant with a truly distinctive identity. The restaurant had these unique features:

- Prices were not fixed. They varied according to the popularity of the dish ordered—just like the stock exchange. The prices of the dishes could be "logged-on" at any time before, during or after the meal.
- The changing prices of the dishes were displayed on a large board.
- The menu was changed daily to provide excitement and speculation.
- The atmosphere was relatively exciting because patrons would not know whether they had made the right choice concerning the prices of the dishes that they had ordered.

8.4 De-organizing The Office

The British advertising agency of Howell Henry Chaldecott Lury & Partners, broke nearly all the rules in the reorganization of its office. The purpose of the reorganization or rather de-*organization* was to boost creativity. Traditional concepts of an office were challenged then dispensed with. Here's what they did:

- The agency's staff were not allocated their own desks. Instead they had to make do with 'hot desks.' That is, using any available desk as the need arose. No fixed abode. No, 'this is my territory."

- Meetings were conducted *standing up* so that they would be over quickly, thereby saving time.
- Traditional office furniture was replaced with brightly colored bean bags. It was believed this would stimulate creativity.
- Laptop computers and mobile phones replaced desktop computers and fixed telephone lines.
- Instead of office decorations using potted plants, a selection of fresh fruit was supplied daily for staff's consumption.
  Another company, Oticon of Denmark, a world leader in hearing-aid manufacture, totally de-organized its office into what the company's president, Lars Kolind, termed as the 'spaghetti organization'. It became an office without a center.

The first step was to auction off all the company's furniture to the employees. Next, walls were taken down, secretaries were eliminated and job descriptions erased. The staff's personal paraphernalia was kept in mobile carts for easy movements.

The company, in effect, became a "100 % project-directed entity" in which its staff identified tasks that needed to be done and formed their own teams accordingly.

The results of this de-organization were *record profits and regaining of its lost market share*. Yes, it sometimes pays to break rules in creative ways!

Mindxercise 8: Challenge The Rules

Many seemingly impossible problems have been solved by challenging the rules. The problems below belong to this category. Why not try out the creativity technique of 'breaking the rules' to solve the following problems?

1. *The farmer's clever daughter*
   A poor farmer was heavily in debt to his rich landlord. The landlord put the debt in abeyance because he was attracted to the farmer's beautiful daughter. However, one day when the farmer was out walking with his daughter, the landlord felt that it was an opportune time to demand payment.

In high spirits, he approached them with a small cloth-bag in his hand. He bent down to pick up two pebbles, which the alert daughter noticed were both black, and made an offer to the farmer. "I'm in a generous mood to—day. I have two pebbles here in my bag, one black and one white. If your beautiful daughter here brings out a white one, all your debts will be written off. If she chooses a black one, your debts will also be written off provided she agrees to marry me." How did the daughter settle the farmer's debt without marrying the landlord?

2. *The unconventional publisher*
   Almost all books in the bookshops appeal to the intellectual capacity of the readers. One publisher decided to buck this trend and built up a flourishing multi-million publishing business. How did he do it?

3. *Body-care products that defy modern technology*
   Nearly all body-care products manufacturers claimed that they were using the latest scientific breakthroughs in the formulation of their products. One woman entrepreneur defied these rules and established a successful network of body-care product shops in many countries. What did she do?

4. *Uncomfortable, heavy and expensive shoes*
   While shoemakers around the world strive to make their shoes increasingly comfortable, a Japanese shoemaker did the opposite.

   Asics Corp makes shoes that are uncomfortable, heavy and expensive. The Shape Walker is shaped to increase the burden of walking on the wearer. Yet these shoes are very popular. Why would people buy such shoes?

5. *Unconventional Product Catalogues*
   What do product catalogues show you? Almost without exception, the companies show their products in the best possible light, literally to perfection. How would you break this rule to create an unconventional catalogue that will attract more customers?

RECORD YOUR
CREATIVITY BLOOM HERE

BRINGING UP CREATIVE CHILDREN

All babies are born with the gift of creativity. Whether this gift develops or not depends very much on how much time parents spend nurturing and stimulating children's learning experiences.

The methods recommended here are those of parents, who have successfully tried them out on their children. They have not been exhausively tested or evaluated by professional child psychologists. Nevertheless, they are very useful and would be a good starting point for you to explore new methods on your own.

Each child is different and possesses his or her own individual temperament and qualities. So read this with an open mind and use your own judgement as a parent to decide whether or not they are relevant and applicable to your child. You may want to record which activities work best with your child. Look for patterns. Generally, the activities suggested here are more appropriate for pre-school children.

Artistic Flair

Children love to explore colors, shapes and patterns. A good way to encourage the youngsters would be to set aside a wall in the house on which they can practice their artistic flair. It is not as outlandish as it sounds. If the wall is painted with gloss paint it will be easy to clean. You can provide them with crayons, color pencils or white board markers and you must clearly explain to them that this is the only wall on which they can write and draw.

You are not (*Jig-word*8*) to be critical of your child's efforts. Remember that their perception as well as hand-eye coordination have not been fully developed. The child's world view and skills are also very different from yours.

A cat, for instance, may look like anything but a cat. Accept your child's explanations for the drawing. Any suggestion must be given in a most positive and encouraging manner. One way to demonstrate your pleasure and pride is to show the artwork to your visiting relatives and friends.

I recall the case of a boy who painted everything a dark and drab grey when his art teacher had given him the assignment of painting a garden scene. The teacher had expected bright and beautiful colors for the flowers and was therefore disappointed with the boy's work. He promptly reprimanded the boy for his inability to translate the garden scene into a colorful painting.

The boy explained that the painting reflected what his garden looked like late in the evening after sunset when everything was drab and grey. Thus from his perception, the boy was absolutely right. Moreover, doing things differently could be a good indication of creativity.

There was another case when a mother forbade her young daughter from bringing home any color pencils or crayons from her kindergarten class. One day, she accidentally discovered that the back of her storeroom door was covered with her daughter's drawings. Only then did she realize that she had been limiting her daughter by depriving her of creative enjoyment.

Development Of Imagination

The development of creative abilities in children does not require expensive materials. In fact, the simpler and less expensive the materials, the better they are for the development of imagination. For instance, children often have much more fun playing with packaging materials of toys rather than with the toys themselves. Cardboard boxes and polystyrene foams provide endless fascination for the child. Such items can become ships, robots, space ships, cars and practically anything that children can imagine.

Origami

Origami or the art of paper folding is yet another inexpensive activity that stimulates the creativity of children. A piece of paper can be transformed into a swan, airplane, boat, dinosaur or a butterfly. Folding papers to create animals and other objects can stimulate the child's imagination for hours. Once they have learnt the basic art of paper folding, it is time to leave them alone to invent their own origami.

Wooden Blocks And Puzzles

Basic wooden blocks and puzzles are also effective ways to develop a child's creativity. Start with a set of a few pieces. As the children improve their skills, add more pieces or buy sets with many pieces. It is even better if you could buy several different sets and mix them together. Though it is good to guide children, it would not be wise to restrict them in the way they manipulate the pieces, especially if they 'stray' from the instructions. In the case of my own experience, my daughter built condominiums, sports stadiums and high-rise buildings even though the set was designed for constructing simple single-story houses only.

Construction Sets

Construction sets like Lego are very effective in bringing out creativity in children. At the familiarization stage, they can follow the standard designs provided by the supplier. Once the children know how to manipulate the different pieces, it is best for them to explore designs of their own. Encourage them to introduce other toy pieces into their construction. Many parents are tempted to exhibit their children's "masterpieces," effectively denying them access to the construction sets. You may display the items for a short period to help your child to develop confidence. However, you will soon want to return the "masterpieces" so that the child can take them apart and construct new designs.

Tidiness

Many parents focus on tidiness that, if carried out with over—zealousness, will discourage creativity in playing with the toys. Do not be overly strict about order for children's toys. Children should be taught to put things back in the right places but this can be done as a form of game or challenge to the child rather than imposing your will on the child. Excessive demand for neatness and order may deter the child from playing with toys or from reading books. Instead, the child may spend more time watching television because there will be nothing to pick up and put away.

Driving

If you drive around with your children in the car, it would be worthwhile to play nursery rhymes and other educational tapes in the car. Sing along with them while driving. In this way, you are not only training your child but also having a wonderful time yourself, despite the traffic jams.

Play games in the car, identifying objects that you pass, such as the various car colors, number plates, trees, buildings, animals and people. Make the trip in your car a new adventure each time.

I created a lot of puzzles when I was travelling with my young children in the car. Some of the examples are below. Can you guess the answers to these sample puzzles that I created for my children?

A. *Passing Objects—What am I?*
    1. What has a goose neck with only one eye?
    2. When one of my eyes turn red, you have to stop
    3. When I blink, you know where I'm going
    4. I'm a giant wheel and when you are near me, you have to stop
    5. Sometimes I'm single. Sometimes I'm double. Sometimes I'm broken. I run parallel to your car.

B. *Things in the Car—What am I?*
    1. When I'm up you can see me. When I'm down you can't see me.
    2. Sometimes your daddy makes me cry when your windshield is dirty
    3. When it is cold outside, I make you warm inside
    4. I'm a pair of ears. I can see but cannot hear.
       I'm like a magic wand that makes your car comes alive.

C. *Parts of your Body—What am I?*
    Two rows of soldiers always matching together with me
    1. A pair of caves whose entrances are blocked by tall grass
    2. A monster that grinds intruders to pieces
    3. You can cut me but I don't feel any pain
    4. You feel happy when I beat you from the inside.

Using your imagination, why not create similar puzzles of your own? Even better still, ask your children, if they are old enough to create such puzzles for you to solve. You will be amazed at their creativity and resourcefulness.

The answers are as below, but I don't think you will need them.
Answers:
    A: 1. Street-lights 2. Red traffic light 3. Signal lights of the car in front
        4. Roundabout 5. White lines on the road
    B: 1. Windows 2. Water-jet 3. Heater 4. Door side rear mirrors 5. Ignition key
    C: Your toes 2. Nostrils 3. Hair and nails 4. Heart

Meal Times

Meal times can be an educational experience too. Explain the use of the cutlery, the different types of crockery and the nutritional values of the food items. Ask your children questions and encourage them to ask questions in return.

Name-Cards

Attach name-cards to items in your house. You will be surprised how fast your children can learn to read. In my case, I hung a world map in my three-year old daughter's room and soon she was able to identify many countries. Her favorite was Australia, which she would proudly point out to me whenever she came across it in magazines, books or signboards.

Garden

The garden is a wonderful place for the children to explore with their senses. Here the child can see, feel, smell, hear and perhaps even sample the taste of fruits and flowers when safe. The sound of birds, insects and wind blowing past their faces completes the sensory exploration. Flowers in particular hold unbounded fascination for children. Take your children to gardens and public parks often.

Supermarket

A trip to the supermarket can be fun for your children. Let them hold small items in their hands. The array of colors and shapes of the packages found there is a dazzling visual experience. Festive decorations will offer even more visual stimulation for children. The idea is to involve them in an endless marvel of the wonderful world around them.

Swimming

Children have a natural attraction to water. The good news is that swimming improves intelligence and fosters creativity. I first learned about this from my eldest daughter. She told me after her first public examination results were announced that all her swimming team-mates did very well. All of them either scored all A's or close to all A's even though they had very little time to study because of their intensive training. My daughter scored all A's herself. She topped her class in school and she was on the Dean's list as one of the top students at a university where she was studying.

I was a bit skeptical at first. That same evening, however, I attended a talk by Dr. Win Wenger, an author and a creativity expert, who was in Kuala Lumpur, Malaysia at that time. That was when I confirmed my daughter's wisdom when she told me about the importance of swimming in promoting intelligence and creativity. Dr. Wenger himself had shot up from a lackluster performance at the bottom of his class to the top of the class after spending several hours of underwater swimming every day in the summer of 1959. He went on to obtain his Ph.D. Dr. Wenger subsequently did extensive research on creativity and has written several books on the subject.

He talked about this method in his book "The Einstein Factor—A Proven New Method for Increasing Your Intelligence".

Dr. Robert Doman, medical director of the Philadelphia Institute for the Achievement of the Human Potential provided an explanation. He explained that underwater swimming increases the carbon dioxide content in the blood. This causes a signal to warn our bodies that our oxygen supply is in danger of being cut off. In response, the carotid arteries that carry blood to our heads dilate and allow more blood to flow through them, saturating our brains in an exceptionally rich flow of oxygenated blood.

It is not my intention to equate creativity with academic performance. I quoted the above cases just to illustrate the effect of mind opening through underwater swimming. School grade in this context is just a convenient manifestation of this mind opening. Generally, school grades, however, may not reflect creativity. They sometimes show the opposite. A grade "A" may prove that one has conformed well.

Swimming is an excellent sport that develops body coordination. All my children are competitive swimmers. Unlike other sports, there is also a minimum risk to injury as the body is well supported by the water. I would recommend that all children take up swimming as it provides all-round physical and mental development.

Communication

As a parent, your communication with your children can be a source of great pleasure and build a marvelous bond to them. Alternately, if done incorrectly, it can be a source of deep distress for everyone and could bring a family to the brink of breakdown or collapse. Spending time with your children, playing, doing interesting things and just hanging out somewhere you both enjoy deepens the quality to your relationship with them.

According to the latest studies, we should praise our children's efforts and improvements but not results. Such praises works best when they are both specific and timely. This will guide them to pursue a much more meaningful purpose-driven life and not a performance-driven life when they grow up. Another finding is that we should not provide incentives for play. Incentives are effective over a short-term. However, over just a short period, play loses its fun and becomes work. In short, you destroy their interest and happiness in their play.

I still remember fondly playing with my four children when they were still young. In fact, my neighbours and visiting relatives commented on my immaturity for playing children's games like hide-and-seek and catching in the garden. I never took notice of such remarks as both my children and I were having a wonderful time together.

During bedtime, I created my own original fictional stories for them (see *Stories* below). In the beginning, I made them super heroes and heroines who saved the world from countless troubles and disasters. Later on, they asked me a lot of Why questions. Since I did not know all the answers, I created my own fairy tales to satisfy their curiosity. At times, I purposely created impossible situations and problems for them to solve. Their imaginative solutions at times absolutely amazed me.

Stories

My youngest daughter when she was about 5-7 years old constantly asked me to tell her bedtime stories on why giraffes have long necks, why crabs walk sideways, why the tortoise has a hard shell, and so on. We lie down together on her bed. She will rest her head in my arm and I created stories for her on the spot! The stories were so interesting to her that sometimes she asked me whether they were real! After the story I will pat her to sleep before leaving her room.

You could do the same. Better still, you could ask your children to create stories for themselves. If you could not do either, then read fairy tales and fantasy stories to stimulate your child's imagination. It is best not to use too highly and colorfully illustrated books as the pictures may stifle their imaginative flights of fantasy.

Let me share two of the stories that I have created for my daughter:

1. How the tortoise got its shell

A long time ago, tortoises resembled squirrels. They were scurrying animals with furless skins.

One day, there was a volcanic eruption and a shell-less tortoise was running for its dear life to escape the flowing lava. Just when it was about to be roasted alive by the molten lava, an eagle from above spied the tortoise as food for its young. With its sharp talons, the eagle swopped downwards and seized the tortoise, just in time to save it from certain death.

The tortoise was glad that it was rescued by the eagle. However, as the eagle flew higher and higher, the tortoise realized that it was taking it to her nest high up in mountain tree. As the eagle approached her nest, the tortoise saw eager young beaks waiting eagerly for their meals. In desperation, the tortoise turned its long neck and bit the eagle's foot. The pain forced the eagle to release its grip on the tortoise and it fell directly onto an unhatched egg.

The force of its fall cracked the egg-shell and caused it to tumbled out of the nest, with the egg-shell still attached to the tortoise's back, down onto the flowing stream of molten lava below. The hot lava sealed the broken egg-shell into a hard-shell permanently attached to the tortoise. There was another eruption throwing the tortoise off the molten lava.

That was how until today, the tortoise has a hard shell with a cracked egg pattern on its back.

2. Why are chillies hot?

A long time ago, chillies are sweet succulent fruits popular with the forest animals. The animals just loved them as they provide both nourishment and enjoyment.

The chilli plants, however, were very worried. They held a discussion. At the rate they were being eaten, the chances of reproducing themselves were very scarce indeed. This caused panic among the plants. They decided to appeal for help.

A rabbit passed by and a chilli plant called out for help. The rabbit stopped and asked, "How can I help?"

The plant explained its situation to the rabbit. The rabbit thought for a while and said "I have no idea, how to help you. Perhaps, the cunning monkey can help."

Just then, a monkey swung by. The chilli plant implored the monkey for help. Scratching its head, the monkey summoned all its cunning to find a solution to the chilli's predicament, but found none.

"Why not asked the wise owl," the monkey suggested and quickly disappeared into the forest to hide its embarrassment.

As the sky darkened, the hooting of the owl could be heard. The chilli plants were ecstatic. They shouted in unison to attract the attention of the wise owl. The owl responded by flying down to the plants to find out the cause of the commotion.

"Wise owl," begged the plants, "please save us from being eaten to extinction." The wise owl listened sympathetically to the plight of the chilli plants. While it was seeking a solution, the sky turned ominous and droplets of rain began to fall from the sky. This triggered an idea in the owl's thoughts.

"I have a solution for you," the owl said gleefully to the anxious plants, "Our friends thunder and lightning will be able to help you."

As thunder and lightning took control of the night sky, the desperate pleadings of the chilli plants could be faintly heard over the din.

"What's going on here?" roared the agitated thunder. After listening to the frightened plants, thunder laughed loudly and called out to its lightning friend.

"Just relax and absorb our joint energies," thunder instructed the plants. With that lightning shot its powerful lightning bolts illuminating the sky. At this signal, thunder gave out its ferocious roar.

As instructed, the chilli plants relaxed themselves to absorb these two tremendous sources of energy. That's why today, when you eat chillies, you can feel the sting of thunder and lightning on your tongue.

Note: *I'm planning a subscription service for my daily original bedtime stories if I could get at least 500 subscribers for a start. So please help me to spread the word around. The first 500 subscribers will be eligible for a special lifetime subscriber fee of only US$7 per month. Email with the title: "Bedtime Stories" to DrYKK@mindbloom.net*

Wonderful Gifts

Remember, children are the most wonderful gifts you have been given. Love, the joy of creativity, and the fun of learning are in turn the best gifts that you can give to your children.

STORIES OF CREATIVITY:

The Boy Who Would Not Be Bullied

A much bigger boy in school was constantly bullying a little boy named John. Butch, the bully warned John not to tell anyone about the bullying. John was scared and did not know what to do. He wanted to tell his teacher and his parents but decided against it. His friends who were similarly bullied by Butch told him that reporting the matter would only make things worse.

John went to bed early after dinner. But he tossed about in his bed unable to fall sleep. He was thinking of ways to overcome his problem with Butch. The thinking tired him but did not offer him any solution. Finally he fell asleep. In his sleep, he dreamt that Butch confronted him in school. Butch was in his usual angry mood. Instead of giving in to Butch or running away as usual, this time John stood his ground. Just when Butch was about to strike him, he (Butch) suddenly disappeared in a puff of smoke!

The dream affected John profoundly when he woke up the next morning. He thought about it on his way to school. The more he thought about it, the more he was convinced that the solution to Butch's bullying was to stand up to him.

During break time, Butch approached John just as he was swallowing his last mouthful of food. But this time, John was ready. When Butch was just within a few steps from him, John confidently drew a line on the ground separating Butch from him. Before Butch could recover from his surprise, John dared him to cross the line!

Butch was not someone who would run away from a challenge. He looked into John's eyes and crossed the line with a puzzled look on his face. As soon as the bully crossed the line, John put on his broadest smile and declared, "Now we are on the same side". With this, he not only won over the bully to be his friend but also had him as a protector during his early years in school.

Mindxercise 9:

Have Fun With Children

I picked up the following Mindxercises from playing with children including my own children. Why don't you try them out yourself and on your children? Have fun and a good time!

1. How do you push a TV through a small hole?
2. What gets dirtier the more you wash it?
3. How do you wrap up fire in a piece of paper?
4. What animal sits when standing, sits when sleeping, sits when sitting?
5. How do you light a match underwater?
6. How do you throw a ball such that it travels as far as it can go, stop and then comes back to you?
7. What has 4 legs when small, 2 legs when big and 3 legs when old?
8. What do you call a deer with no eyes?

9. You have (ten) 10 oranges on a table. You took two. How many do you have?

10. A 6 km. long bridge can take a maximum load of three (3) tons only.

   A truck weighing exactly 3 tons started its journey from one end of the bridge. When it traveled halfway through the bridge, a bird landed on the truck. Will the bridge collapse?

RECORD YOUR
CREATIVITY BLOOM HERE

NURTURING YOUR OWN CREATIVITY

We are apt to think that our ideas are the creation of our own wisdom but the truth is that they are the result of the experience through outside contact.

Konosuke Matsushita

Leave the beaten track occasionally and dive into the woods. You will be certain to find something you have never seen before.

Alexander Graham Bell

All of us are born creative but as we grow older we tend to neglect our naturally endowed creativity. We can bring our creative powers back if we really wanted to. This book will hopefully spur you on in this quest.

The simple activities below come from my own personal experience, which I would like to share with you. Try out those you feel comfortable with and experiment with others of your own. Remember there's really no right or wrong method. Try not to be too ambitious and try a little at a time. In due course they will become second nature to you and you will begin to enjoy the exploration of your creativity.

Breaking Routines

For most of us, our lives are governed by routines. We go to work at about the same time every working day, drive along the same route and probably get caught in the early morning traffic daily. I suggest that you break some of these routines.

Occasionally, get up half an hour earlier than usual and enjoy a slow leisurely drive. Try to be more observant this time. You will see things that you have missed before such as a restaurant, a provision shop or even a florist depending what your area of interest is. If you are like me, you may even discover services that you have been looking for all along, such as a barbershop that you pass by everyday but failed to notice. There may be other interesting features, ornamental plants, flower species, sidewalk advertisements that begin to attract your attention.

Another way to break your routine is to use a different route to work. Getting lost or ending up in a dead-end alley could be one of the risks. However, if you view this positively, it could provide a whole new and refreshing experience. For example, the route could be longer but the drive could be much more pleasant and may enable you to escape the usual traffic jams. You may see new surroundings which you never knew existed before. Moreover, venturing into the unknown will put a sense of adventure and excitement into your life.

Play With Young Children

Observing the spontaneity, the simplicity, the innocence and the imagination of children at play is to me one of life's most pleasurable experiences. Of course, playing with them is even better. I am talking about pre-school and kindergarten children. I still play hide-and seek with my five-year old daughter and share with her some of her fantasies.

Some people find it unacceptable behavior for a fully-grown adult to frolic and play with young children. But I can assure you that it is an invigorating experience. There's nothing like feeling young again. Be warned, however, that it can be a tiring experience.

Initially, you may feel a bit strange and uncomfortable but the best way to join in the fun is to get down to their level and to be accepted by them, which is not an easy thing to do. Some adults are afraid that playing with them could cause discipline problems with their children. There's no need to worry too much about this as children instinctively know the limits, even though they have to be reminded at times.

Cartoons, Jokes & Puzzles

Cartoons, jokes and puzzles are the gems of creativity, which keep us amused and entertained. Political satire appearing in magazines such as Newsweek and Time convey interesting but sometimes subtle messages which frequently remind us of the folly of human nature. In Malaysia, Lat's cartoons are a must if we want to understand the idiosyncrasies of Malaysian culture.

The cartoon strips appearing in our daily newspapers carry interesting interpretations of human behavior, sometimes effectively conveyed by having animals taking on human characteristics. These instantly bring to mind the irrepressible cat, Garfield, the writer dog Snoopy (Peanuts) and Calvin's constant companion, Hobbes, the tiger. These cartoons and jokes generally have one thing in common; they convey the punch line at the end. They are real works of creativity as the message comes out within a single cartoon strip.

Puzzles are yet another category of creative works that can keep us occupied for hours. They are good training for the mind as they teach us to look at a problem from different perspectives.

Read Outside Your Scope Of Work

I find reading to be the best source of knowledge and it is perfect for filling in time-slots between appointments and other duties. In order to be creative, it is important to read as wide a range of books as possible and not confine ourselves to books and magazines or journals relating to our professions.

Short feature articles in newspapers covering a wide range of issues provide good reading materials. Sunday papers in particular are my favorite and it is hard for me to pass my weekend without going through them. Sometimes browsing through magazines in which we have no special interest can be rewarding as it makes us be aware of things, which we might otherwise not notice. The bookshop is a good place for getting really good great ideas.

Pay Attention To Advertisements

It has been said that the most expensive movies ever made in terms of cost per second are the TV and cinema advertisements. Their unit production cost even exceeds those of cinema blockbuster movies with high-tech special effects.

A lot of creativity is put into these advertisement productions, usually only 30-seconds long. It is worthwhile paying attention to them and appreciating the efforts that have been put in. The same applies to advertisement in the printed media like magazines and newspapers. So next time when you watch a film or a TV program pay heed on the creative inputs involved. Slogans and catchy phrases in the printed media are also interesting works of creativity.

Carry A Notebook

Always carry a paper notebook or an electronic device like a smart mobile phone or an iPad with you. You never know when it will become handy in jotting down ideas that pop into your head. It's also useful to jot down ideas from what other people said, from publications or just plain observations. The mere act of recording something helps to register the idea in your mind. They then become part of the pool of resources which you can draw upon to make connections.

Surf The Internet

The internet provides a rich and inexhaustible source of creative ideas. Spend time to familiarize yourself with the Google search engine. Learn to use the specific features, including its advance features. By using the Google Alert feature, you don't have to look for information; you can have the most up-to-date information looking for you!

Blogs, ezines, the video channel YouTube (www.YouTube.com), interest groups like Yahoo and Google Groups and of course the biggest social network ever created, Facebook (www.facebook.com).

My personal favorite video channel is TED (Technology, Engineering and Design). Every video show is limited to 18 minutes and from my personal experience, every one of the videos is a gem.

Finally, keep an open mind and be tolerant and receptive of the other person's viewpoints. Creativity is a skill that can be cultivated and nurtured.

RECORD YOUR
CREATIVITY BLOOM HERE

TEN COMMANDMENTS FOR CORPORATE CREATIVITY

"No innovation, no competitiveness—that is the challenge of the new millennium . . . . We need more people with creative minds to be competitive. Our societies must discourage imitation and provide incentives to make products with originality."

Stan Shih, Chairman & CEO, Acer Group

Detailed long-range planning coupled with tight control at the center is a remarkably effective way of killing creativity and entrepreneurship at the extremities of the organization, the individuals who make it up.

Kenichi Ohmae

Creativity is the foundation of business success though its impact is not obvious. This is because what is obvious now started as an innovation by a creative entrepreneur. The concept of multi—level marketing by Amway; the promotion of computers for personal use at home by Apple computers; designating watches as popular fashion wear items by the Swiss watch company, Swatch; the franchising of food by McDonalds; merchandising over the internet by Amazon.com; the list goes on and on. They are obvious to us now but they all started as innovations.

Successful companies that achieve and sustain impressive growth and profits tend to be characterized by a corporate culture in which innovation thrives at all levels. The first step in innovation is creativity. Creativity comes from treating workers at all levels as a set of brains rather than a pair of hands.

Many companies have set up their own creative and innovation centers to drive creativity in their organizations. The multinational company DuPont, for example, has set up an official DuPont Center for Creativity and Innovation. As a testimony to the success of this center, the employees themselves established on a volunteer basis the DuPont Oz Creative Thinking Network. This network is devoted to educating themselves and others in the field of creativity and innovation and applying the learning's to practical on-the-job issues.

Nowadays, companies are tapping into the power of the internet to leverage their innovation capacity. Looking outside the confines of the company's employees for innovation is referred to as *Open Innovation.*

Open Innovation is a term coined by Henry Chesbrough in his book *Open Innovation: The new imperative for creating and profiting from technology.* It taps into the wisdom of crowds such as external experts, consumers, suppliers and the general public for ideas and solutions.

There are two main types of Open Innovation:

Crowdsourcing is about outsourcing a job to an undefined, generally large group of people external to the organization. It could be in the form of a promotion, competition or an open invitation to the public for feedback and ideas.

Crowdcasting is a strategy in which a corporation disseminates details of a specific problem or situation to a specially selected group of people, for example experts, for possible solutions. The process is often conducted as a competition. It is usually used to seek solutions to more challenging issues. I have been involved as a judge in the *Innovation Challenge*, the largest MBA innovation competition in the world. The competition is sponsored by major companies keen to harvest the ideas of MBA students to come out with new innovative solutions.

Based on my study of successful innovative companies, I have made a compilation of their successful systems into a simple practical guide for you to explore for possible adaptation and implementation in your organization. I called them the *INNOVATIVE Guide for Corporate Creativity* (easily remembered by the acronym—**INNOVATIVE**).

The guide below is people-centred, mainly focused on employees. It is wise to expand the scope to open-innovation by harnessing the power of the internet, whenever and wherever it is feasible to do so.

Innovative Guide For Corporate Creativity

1. Institute Creativity Awards
2. Nurture staff's creativity
3. Notify results of suggestions received
4. Organize an Annual Family Creativity Festival.
5. Value Copycats
6. Allow a cooling off period
7. Train staff in creativity skills
8. Implement a Mistake of the Month Award
9. View results of creativity by measurement tools.
10. Encourage free association

1. Institute Creativity Awards

Recognition is one of the most powerful motivating factors for any individual. Institute the Best Idea of the Month Award for the entire organization. According to research findings, very often the best ideas come from frontline workers.

There was a case when a worker passed by an automobile assembly line and something struck him as being odd. The line has been operating for more than a year and hundreds if not thousands of people passed by without noticing anything unusual. The unusual thing was that the entire robotic assembly line was fully lighted with powerful down lights! Unlike human workers, the robots do not need lights to operate. By bringing out this fact to the management, the worker saved thousands of dollars per month in electricity cost. The worker was promptly recognized as the recipient of the Best Idea of the Month Award.

Linus Pauling, the Nobel laureate said that to get one good idea you have to get plenty of new ideas. Quantity of ideas is very important as they have a tendency to cross-pollinate, resulting in great and practical ideas. Encourage the endless flow of ideas—the crazier the better as they are useful in breaking paradigms and mindsets. Instituting the Most Ideas of the Month Award without regard to their practicality is an excellent way to get the ideas gushing in your organization.

2. Nurture Staff's Creativity

An essential requirement to nurture your staff's creativity is the ability to recognize when good rules become bad ones—and the foresight, creativity and imagination to challenge them. Bureaucratic procedures that serve the company in the past may become an impediment to creativity.

Managing the imagination of your people is much more important than managing the organization structure and the company's equipment or hardware. Empowerment is a powerful tool. Jan Carlzon was able to transform the SAS (Scandinavian Airlines) from a loss making, bureaucratic—centered organization to a customer—obsessed company run by empowered frontline personnel. He coined the term, *"Moments of Truth"* to describe every moment of contact of the personnel with a customer. They were encouraged to solve problems on the spot using their own ingenuity. This creative empowerment transformed SAS into one of the top performing airlines in Europe.

3. Notify Results Of Suggestions Received

Studies have indicated that suggestion boxes and other forms of feedback from employees are ineffective because it was perceived that the management was not serious about the suggestions submitted. This problem was successfully resolved by making it the management's responsibility to respond within a specified time frame. If no response is received within the specified time frame, make it a policy that the suggestion submitted has been automatically approved for implementation. This places the onus of response on the management which will go a long way in winning credibility from the staff.

Based on the figures published by the *National Annual Report on Japanese Kaizen Teian Systems*, the Japanese company Idemitsu Kosan received 1,073,256 ideas over a period of one year and emerged as the champion with an average of 118.3 ideas per employee. This was made possible by notifying staff on the results of their suggestions and taking steps to implement them wherever feasible.

4. Organize An Annual Family Creativity Festival

There are undiscovered talents in every organization. An Annual Family Creativity Festival provides a fantastic opportunity to uncover such talents. Creativity blossoms in an atmosphere of fun and freedom. Instead of spending lots of money to employ professional entertainers, the money is allocated to Fun Teams to come out with crazy inventions of their own liking. Each team has to work out their own budget and their plans for the budget. The resulting invention is paraded in an open ground together with other games and festivities. There should also be plenty of food cooked and served by members of the employees' families. Almost everything is done in-house, except perhaps for the building of booths, canopies and basic infrastructure for the festivities.

Instead of a family festival, IBM organises an annual *Innovation Jam* since 2001 to tap into the creativity of its worldwide employees and selected outsiders who are dispersed worldwide. The winning ideas can get funding, the contributors of the ideas are not rewarded directly. The average annual funding to develop the shortlisted ideas is $100 million.

5. Value Copycats

The *"not invented here"* is a prevalent syndrome in many large organizations. There is a tendency to reject ideas and innovations from external sources. This is particularly so when a garage style one-man operation comes out with a discovery or innovation which stumps an entire R&D department staffed by highly paid and highly qualified professionals with a big budget.

The pioneer of photocopying machines, Rank Xerox found itself in deep trouble when Japanese firms like Canon were able to produce and sell such machines at a much lower cost than Xerox. In fact, Canon's selling price for fax machines were even lower than that Xerox's production cost. Sales were dropping rapidly and Xerox was desperate to find a solution. In their bid to turn around, Xerox pioneered the concept of "bench-marking". This essentially means to study the best practices of other organizations and where applicable incorporate such practices into their own organization. This "Copycat" strategy effectively saved Xerox from impending disaster and enabled Xerox to continue its path of growth.

Sam Walton, the founder of Wal-Mart, the largest supermarket retail chain in the US attributed his success to his supreme devotion to copying the best practices of other stores. He said: *"Almost everything I've done, I copied from someone else."*

The multinational corporation, Raychem openly promotes the stealing of ideas. It created two awards for the person who copies the idea and the person who provided the idea within the organization. The award is in the form of trophy and certificate. The certificate for the '*idea stealer*" reads: *"I stole somebody's idea and I'm using it."* The originator of the idea gets a certificate that says: "I had a great idea and—is using it."

Note: I have developed a 7-step process for Copycat Innovation that provides you with a measurable results-driven fast-track innovation that optimizes success by minimising risk, time and resources. If you are keen to know more about this process, please send me an email to DrYKK@mindbloom.net with the title "Copycat" to get a free copy of my report: "Copycat Innovation: The Unbeatable Ethical Route to Profitable Innovation".

6. Allow A Cooling-Off Period

Sometimes it is dangerous to approve an idea if it is too enthusiastically endorsed unanimously by those present at a meeting. The danger is that the meeting could be locked in a one-track thinking path. This is especially true if the originator of the idea is someone in a senior position. Robert Townsend in his book: "Down the Organization" says that if everyone agrees too readily with an idea it is probably because that is what the meeting wants to hear. The great steel magnate Andrew Carnegie had a policy that if everyone agreed with an idea, he would put off decision making to allow for a cooling-off period to re-examine the idea. He found that very often, the original idea was not a very good one after all and a better solution was found upon reflection of the original idea.

7. Train Staff In Creativity Skills

Creativity experts like Edward de Bono believe that creativity is a skill that can be taught. In fact all of us are born creative. It is the need to conform to social norms that stifles creativity. We can rekindle the creativity spark in us through training as much more is known about the brain during the last decade than the entire human civilization before it. There are specific techniques which can enhance and unleash our inherent creativity. The five steps and three primary techniques outlined in this book could be used to unleash your creativity. Training coupled with a creativity culture will bring out the best from the people in your organization.

Note:
- If you are interested to having me to conduct a creativity/innovation workshop for your organisation, please email me with the title: Workshop" to DrYKK@mindbloom.net
- If you would like to subscribe to free Business Innovation Digest enewsletter, please send an email to DrYKK@mindbloom.net with the title:" BID"

8. Implement A Mistake Of The Month Award

Success in business comes from making the right decisions. Making the right decisions requires experience. Experience comes from making mistakes. Therefore a culture for tolerating mistakes is an essential part of business success. Moreover, making mistakes is also part and parcel of a culture for innovation.

A story was told of a senior engineer who made a $20 million mistake at IBM. He was waiting for a summon from his boss Tom Watson to mete out his punishment for the mistake made. When the engineer was finally summoned to see the boss after what seemed like an interminable wait, the engineer was prepared for the worst. Instead, Tom never mentioned the mistake to him at all. All he did was to brief the engineer on a new project and asked him to lead it. The engineer could not control his anxiety anymore and asked his boss as to when he would be fired from his job. *"Fire you from the job after a $20 million experience? No way!"* was Watson's prompt response. The engineer stayed on to become one of IBM's most valuable staff.

Another story relates to Henry Ford. One of his vice-presidents made a huge inventory error costing the company more than $1 million, a lot of money in 1920. Expecting to be fired from his job, the VP submitted his resignation to Ford. Ford read the letter and tore it up on the spot.

"Do you think I would fire you after what has just happened?" he asked. *"I have just invested $1 million in your education!"* The VP stayed on to help make Ford Motors into a highly profitable automobile company.

9. View Results Of Creativity By Measurement Tools

It is possible to quantify savings or earnings based on innovation. In the example of the Best Idea Award (see No.1 above), the value of the idea of saving electricity by switching off the lighting in the robotic assembly section was easily measurable.

The American Airlines saved more than half a million dollars from a simple idea from its lead flight attendant. Her idea was to provide first class passengers with two 100gm caviar cans rather than the usual one 200gm can as she observed a lot of wastage. This idea reduced the airline's annual consumption of $3 million by over half a million dollars.

Not all creativity can be measured but an attempt should be made to quantify its value wherever possible as it serves as a real morale booster for the staff. Of course, a portion of the value should be distributed back as incentives.

10. Encourage Free Association

Casual conversations among employees are potent weapons for making technological breakthroughs. Two engineers who had just finished their design of the engine for HP's new laser printer were having coffee when they were joined by their other colleagues. They talked about the type of printer they would like to have if they could have anything they wanted. The consensus was to have a color printer with a resolution of at least 200 dots per inch. The two development engineers could not get this idea out of their mind. They made a connection with the way coffee percolators worked and tried heating up the ink. The result was a controlled ink explosion and they invented the highly successful inkjet printer. This would not have happened if not for the casual conversation at the coffee machine.

Such incidents of breakthroughs are by no means isolated. In fact, it seems to be the most effective mechanism for innovations and is popularly practiced in the Silicon Valley.

Nurturing a creativity culture is a necessity if companies and organizations are to survive and grow as they pass into the next millennium. It is worthwhile to remember that a bad system beats a good person anytime. Conversely, a good system provides a conducive environment for the flowering of creativity and profitability.

Wave Of Innovation

The *DuPont Center For Creativity & Innovation* has established the Wave of Innovation Award to innovators in the DuPont company. The following words provided inspiration to the staff:

Upon the vast ocean of resources, Creativity and innovation rise.
A resounding, perpetual motion, pressed by the constant winds of change.
New ideas rush to meet each other—taking shape
And setting into motion a new wave
Of creativity and innovation
The wave steadily sweeps across the ocean, quickly gaining momentum
and strength; improving; growing; redefining its shape.
Soon the wave crests with the force of innovative change, exploding and
releasing an energy that uncovers
New resources—new areas of growth and improvement. And then,
the wave quickly flows back into the ocean;
This time with a different kind of energy; an energy that will
Help create the next wave of innovation.

RECORD YOUR
CREATIVITY BLOOM HERE

FURTHER BLOOM: THE BIKINI TECHNIQUE

This book uses the bikini technique—it is short and brief but covers all the essentials. There are dozens or even hundreds of creativity techniques but I believe that it is neither necessary nor important to learn about all of them. What is important is to be able to grasp the basic principles, which is what this book is all about.

All creativity techniques have one thing in common; that is to help us make connections. Creativity will come naturally once we master the art of observation and making connections through our daily experiences. Nevertheless, it is still necessary to resort to specific creativity techniques in solving difficult problems.

The *Five Steps to Creativity* coupled with the *Three Primary Creativity Techniques* provide you with the fundamental tools to creativity.

All creativity techniques are useless unless and until you apply them. Conditioning our minds to creative thinking through the techniques outlined in this book will immeasurably enhance and enrich your life and those of others around you.

However, do not feel constrained by them as this defeats the very purpose of creativity. Once you understand the significance of the techniques and are familiar with them, it is time to explore and develop techniques of your own. All that matters is that they work for you.

Creative Thinking

The famous creativity expert Edward de Bono says that creativity can be taught and is a skill that we can all learn:

"Creative thinking is like driving a car, juggling, cooking, skiing, playing darts or knitting. Some people will be better than others but everyone can acquire a reasonable amount of skill with practice. It starts with desire, then comes attention, practice and finally enjoyment. At the beginning, there is a certain degree of awkwardness and the activity seems both unnecessary and unnatural. Once you get used to it, creativity thinking becomes a natural process like riding a bicycle or swimming."

All that you need to do is to practice creative thinking frequently and you can become a creative person.

Creative Person

What is a Creative Person? Mike Vance and Dianne Deacon in their book: "Think Out Of The Box", provided an excellent description:

"The creative person is one who harnesses the creative process in pursuing the greatest art form of all—meaningful living. The creative person achieves personal fulfillment through participation in life's most rewarding activity—productive thought. The creative person enjoys the beauty and warmth of the rising sun, envisions the potential of the human race, hurls artificial orbiting stars into the sky, cares for little children, builds birds sanctuaries by the water edge and contemplates what is in the darkness beyond the night."

Most Beautiful Experience

Albert Einstein provided a further elaboration of a creative person. According to him, a creative person is able to enjoy the most beautiful experience—the mystery of the universe.

"The most beautiful experience we can have is the mysterious. It is the fundamental emotion, which stands at the cradle of true art and true science. He to whom the emotion is a stranger, who can

no longer pause and stand wrapped in awe, is as good as dead; his eyes are closed.

The most important thing is not to stop questioning. Curiosity has its own reason for existing. One cannot help but be in awe when one contemplates the mysteries of eternity, of life, of the marvelous structure of reality. It is enough if one tries merely to comprehend a little of this mystery every day. Never lose a holy curiosity."

Albert Einstein

Success

Make your creative thinking as one of your main tools to achieve success in your life. But do you know exactly what success is? Perhaps the words of the famous writer Ralph Waldo Emerson will offer you some food for thought:

"To laugh often and much; to win the respect of intelligent people and the affection of children; to earn the appreciation of honest critics and endure the betrayal of false friends; to appreciate beauty; to find the best in others; to leave the world a bit better whether by a healthy child, a garden patch, or a redeemed social condition; to know even one life has breathed easier because you have lived. This is to have succeeded."

Ralph Waldo Emerson

Another interpretation of success is by Robert Louis Stevenson:

"He has achieved success who has lived well, laughed often, and loved much; who has gained the respect of intelligent men and the love of little children; who has filled his niche and accomplished his task, who has left the world better than he found it, whether by an improved poppy, a perfect poem, or a rescued soul; who has never lacked appreciation of earth's beauties, nor failed to express it; who has always looked for the best in others and given the best he had; whose life is an inspiration; whose memory a benediction."

Robert Louis Stevenson

A Better World

Finally, let us examine the impact of creativity on the world. Alex Osborn, the inventor of the most popular creativity technique "Brainstorming" has this to say:

> *"It is now a well known fact that nearly all of us can become more creative, if we will. And this very fact may well be the hope of the world. By becoming more creative we can lead brighter lives, and can live better with each other. By becoming more creative we can provide better goods and services to each other, to the result of a higher and higher standard of living. By becoming more creative we may even find a way to bring permanent peace to all the world."*

Alex Osborne

In the words of Nelson Mandela, during his inauguration address as the first non-white President of South Africa:

> *Our deepest fear is not that we are inadequate*
> *Our deepest fear is that we are powerful beyond measure It is our light,*
> *not our darkness, that most frightens us We ask ourselves:*
> *Who am I to be brilliant, gorgeous, talented and fabulous?*
> *Actually who are you not to be? You are a child of God.*
> *Your playing small doesn't serve the world There is nothing enlightened*
> *about shrinking so that other people won't feel insecure about you.*
> *We are born to manifest the glory of God that is within us.*
> *It is not just in some of us: it's in everyone.*
> *And as we let our own light shine, we unconsciously give other people*
> *permission to do the same.*
> *As we are liberated from our own fear, our presence automatically*
> *liberates others.*

You are creative. Let your creativity bloom.

QUOTES ON CREATIVITY

Action

Vision without action is merely a dream. Action without vision just passes the time. Vision with action can change the world!

Joel Arthur Barker

What you can do, or dream you can, begin it; boldness has genius, power and magic in it.

Goethe

Held in the palms of thousands of disgruntled people over the centuries have been ideas worth millions—if they only had taken the first step and then followed through.

Robert M. Hayes

Brain

Natural resources have dropped out of the competitive equation. In fact, a lack of natural resources may even be an advantage. Because the industries we are competing for—the industries of the future—are all based on brainpower.

Lester Thurow

The brain is a wonderful organ; it starts the moment you get up in the morning and does not stop until you get to the office.

Robert Frost

The more you use your brain, the more brain you will have to use.

George A. Dorsey

Change

If we do not change fast enough, we're going to miss so many chances . . . change means the abandonment of rules which have served us well.

Lee Kuan Yew

Children
Children between the ages of two and seven are very imaginative. This is the best period for the development of imagination, creativity and thinking abilities.

Chiam Heng Keng

Focus should be to encourage and develop creativity in all children without the ultimate goal being to make all children inventors, but rather to develop a future generation of critical thinkers.

Faraq Mousa

Creativity provides an exciting way for children to become intrinsically motivated, to find joy in the ordinary, and to discover their hidden talents. All children possess creativity.

Steve Dahlberg

Parents should realize that it is better to bring children up as excited innovators and thinkers instead of unhappy and obedient followers.

Chong Sheau Ching

Creativity and the arts are important for all children throughout their lives no matter what field they go into.

Gloria Estafan

Creation
The whole difference between construction and creation is exactly this: that a thing is constructed can only be loved after it is constructed; but a thing created is loved before it exists.

Charles Dickens

We are apt to think that our ideas are the creation of our own wisdom but the truth is that they are the result of the experience through outside contact.

Konosuke Matsushita

The creation of a thousand forests is in one acorn.

Ralph Waldo Emerson

Creativity
Creativity is a characteristic given to all human beings at birth.

Abraham Maslow

Creativity is inventing, experimenting, growing, taking risks, breaking rules, making mistakes and having fun.

Mary Lou Cook

To be consistently creative is to be empowered. There is nothing that can truly secure a better future for you than having the ability to be creative at will, to solve problems, and develop new concepts whenever required.

Marsh Fisher

We may discover that creativity is a common business trait.

Isaac Asimov

Being creative would be so much easier if it weren't for all those people who become or think they are "instant experts" on any and all topics, who get up in the morning simply to "kill" our ideas.

R. Alan Black

All of us are creative; we vary only to the extent to which we have developed our creativity potential.

Arthur B. Van Gundy

Creativity isn't an option anymore. It's not just a skill needed in traditional creative careers, but very much a part of all aspects of business today.

Lim Kok Wing

Curiosity
God spare me sclerosis of the curiosity, for the curiosity which craves to keep us informed about the small things no less than the large is the mainspring, the dynamo, the jet propulsion of all complete living.

John Mason Brown

Dream
If a little dreaming is dangerous, the cure for it is not to dream less but to dream more, to dream all the time.

Marcel Proust

Economy
In the new economy strategic resources no longer come out of the ground. The strategic resources are ideas and information that come out of our minds.

John Sculley

Entrepreneurship
Detailed long-range planning coupled with tight control at the center is a remarkably effective way of killing creativity and entrepreneurship at the extremities of the organization, the individuals who make it up.

Kenichi Ohmae

Eureka !
A moment's insight is sometimes worth a life's experience.

Oliver Wendell Holmes

I can remember the very spot in the road, whilst in my carriage, when to my joy the solution occurred to me.

Charles Darwin

Anything that increases the stress on a system leads to a jump to a higher level of being. Instead of breaking down physically, you jump through a creative Eureka! Experience into a higher state of mind.

Ilya Prigogine

Detailed long-range planning coupled with tight control at the center is a remarkably effective way of killing creativity and entrepreneurship at the extremities of the organization, the individuals who make it up.

Kenichi Ohmae

Genius
All children are born geniuses, and we spend the first six years of their lives degeniusing them.

Buckminster Fuller

Gifted
The most gifted member of the human species are at their best when then they cannot have their way.

Erik Hoffer

History

History is but the story of the achievements of people who had creative imagination.

Sidney Newton Bremer

Ideas

The man with a new idea is a crank—until the idea succeeds.

Mark Twain

A person who can create ideas worthy of note is a person who has learned much from others.

Konosuke Matsushita

The best way to get a good idea is to get a lot of ideas.

Linus Pauling

No idea is so outlandish that it should not be considered with a searching but at the same time steady eye.

Winston Churchill

It is easier to tone down a wild idea than to think up a new one.

Alex Osborne

The good ideas are all hammered out in agony by individuals, not spewed out by groups.

Charles Brower

All achievements, all earned riches, have their beginning in an idea.

Napoleon Hill

"Every revolutionary idea seems to evoke three stages of reaction. They may be summed up by the phrases: (1) It's completely impossible. (2) It's possible, but it's not worth doing. (3) I said it was a good idea all along."

Arthur C. Clarke

Imagination

To raise new questions, new possibilities, to regard old problems from a new angle requires a creative imagination and marks the real advances in science.

Albert Einstein

DR. YKK

Imagination is more important than knowledge.

Albert Einstein

Every great advance in science has issued from a new audacity of imagination.

John Dewey

Imagination is the beginning of creation.

George Bernard Shaw

What is now proved was once only imagined.

William Blake

Imagination is the living power and prime agent of all human perception.

Samuel Taylor Coleridge

A man to carry on a successful business must have imagination. He must see things in a vision, a dream of the whole thing.

Charles M. Schwab

The sorcery and charm of imagination, and the power it gives to the individual to transform his world into a new world of order and delight, makes it one of the most treasured of all human capacities.

Frank Barron

He who has imagination without learning has wings and no feet.

Joseph Joubert

Imagination grows by exercise, and contrary to common belief, is more powerful in mature than in the young.

W. Somerset Maugham

The world is but a canvas to our imaginations.

Henry David Thoreau

Microsoft is a company that manages imagination.

Bill Gates

The human race built most nobly when the limitations were greatest; therefore when most is required of imagination to build it all.

Frank Lloyd Wright

Impact
Ideas shape the course of history.

John Maynard Keynes

The profit of great ideas comes when you turn them into reality.

Tom Hopkins

Greater than the tread of mighty armies is an idea whose time has come.

Victor Hugo

There is no doubt that creativity is the most important human resource of all. Without creativity, there would be no progress, and we would be forever repeating the same patterns.

Edward de Bono

Creative thinking is not a talent, it is a skill that can be learnt. It empowers people by adding strength to their natural abilities which improves teamwork, productivity and where appropriate profits.

Edward de Bono

The more you think, the more time you have

Henry Ford

Innovation
No innovation, no competitiveness—that is the challenge of the new millennium. . . . We need more people with creative minds to be competitive. Our societies must discourage imitation and provide incentives to make products with originality.

Stan Shih

Knowledge
Knowledge is being applied to knowledge itself. It is now fast becoming the one factor in production, sidelining both capital and labour.

Peter Drucker

Where is the wisdom that we have lost in knowledge? Where is the knowledge we have lost in information?

T. S. Elliot

Mind

The creative mind doesn't have to have the whole pattern—it can have just a little piece and be able to envision the whole picture in completion.

Arthur Fry

The mind is not a vessel to be filled but a fire to be sparked.

Plutarch

My advice to any young person at the beginning of their career is to try to look for the mere outlines of big things with their fresh, untrained and unprejudiced mind.

Hans Selye

The mind of man is like a clock that is always running down, and requires to be constantly wound up.

William Hazlitt

The most powerful factors in the world are clear ideas in the minds of energetic men of good will.

J. Arthur Thompson

Many have original minds who do not think it—they are led away by custom.

John Keats

It is not enough to have a good mind. The main thing is to use it well.

Rene Descartes

Iron rusts from disuse, stagnant water loses its purity and in cold weather becomes frozen; even so does inaction saps the vigours of the mind.

Leonardo da Vinci

Non-conformity

Let us not follow where the path may lead. Let us go instead where there's no path and leave a trail.

Japanese Proverb

Leave the beaten track occasionally and dive into the woods. You will be certain to find something you have never seen before

Alexander Graham Bell

Creativity often rewards the non-conformist, the iconoclast, the generalist who treats life not as a linear fast track to success, but as a forest of rich discoveries that one can meander through, creating one's own trail.

Ho Kwon Ping

The creative person prefers the richness of the disordered to the stark barrenness of the simple.

Donald W. MacKinnon

The common cliché is "get real". Our watchword will be "get bizzare". Real solutions to problems (true creativity) comes from fantasy rather than from file cabinet in our head.

Fred M. Amran

Detecting the wrong answer requires intelligence. To be able to ask the right question requires creativity.

Anonymous

Nurturing Creativity

I consider it my job to nurture the creativity of the people I work with because at Sony we know that a terrific idea is more likely to happen in an open, free and trusting atmosphere than when everything is calculated, every action analysed and every responsibility assigned by an organisation chart.

Akio Morita

The most important thing is not to stop questioning. Curiosity has its own reason for existing. One cannot help but be in awe when he contemplates the mysteries of eternity, of life, of the marvellous structure of reality. It is enough if one tries merely to comprehend a little of this mystery every day. Never lose a holy curiosity.

Albert Einstein

Go ahead and be whacky. Get into a crazy frame of mind and ask what's funny about what you're doing.

Roger von Oech

Your most brilliant ideas come in a flash, but the flash comes only after a lot of hard work.

Edward Blakeslee

Creative activity increases creative ability.

Harry Lorayne
Neville Smith

The human mind treats a new idea the way the body treats a strange protein; it rejects it.

P.B. Medawar

A good idea is the enemy of a better one. You stop looking for alternatives.

Tudor Rickards

An idea's worth is directly proportional to the opposition created.

Robert Townsend

Organizations

The organizations of the future will increasingly depend on the creativity of their members to survive. Great Groups offer a new model in which the leader is an equal among Titans. In a truly creative collaboration, work is pleasure, and the only rules and procedures are those that advance the common cause.

Warren Bennis

The things we fear most in organizations—fluctuations, disturbances, imbalances—are the primary source of creativity.

Margaret Wheatly.

Potential

If I have seen further it is by standing on the shoulders of giants.

Isaac Newton

An essential aspect of creativity is not being afraid to fail.

Edwin Land

Everything of importance has been seen by someone who did not discover it.

Alfred North Whitehead

Compared to what we ought to be, we are only half awake. We are making use of only a small part of our mental resources.

William James

Process
The creative process is a matter of continually separating and bringing together, bringing together and separating, in many dimensions—affective, conceptual, perceptual, volitional and physical.

Albert Rothenberg

A creative moment is part of a longer creative process which, in turn, is part of a creative life.

Tom Wujec

No matter how old you get, if you can keep the desire to be creative, you're keeping the man-child alive.

John Cassavetes

Problem
No problem can withstand the assault of sustained thinking.

Voltaire

Prosperity
Ultimately creativity becomes the cornerstone for the organization's rejuvenation, growth and prosperity.

Leonard M.S. Yong

Creativity and innovation are crucial to sustain rapid economic growth.

Datuk Law Hieng Ding

Quality
The quality of an organization can never exceed the quality of the minds that make it up.

Harold R. McAlindon.

Sex
Sex and creativity are often seen by dictators as subversive activities.

Erica Jong

Sex energy is the creative energy of all geniuses. There never has been, and never will be a great leader, builder or artist lacking in the driving force of sex.

Napoleon Hill

Creativity as the "sex of our mental lives." Ideas, like organisms, have a life cycle, they are born, they develop, they reach maturity and they die. So we need a way to generate new ideas. Creative thinking is the means and like its biological counterpart, it is also pleasurable.

Roger von Oech

Strategy

Strategy is about setting yourself apart from the competition. It's not a matter of being better at what you do—it's a matter of being different at what you do

Michael Porter

I believe that the beginning of strategy is a contrarian nature. Somebody who is willing to challenge the existing wisdom, challenge the assumption base, and turn it on its head and say, "Now, what do we have here?"

Gary Hamel

Thinking

The mind ought to sometimes be diverted that it may return the better to thinking.

Phaedrus

Don't let assumptions, conventions and traditions hold you back or cloud your thinking.

Guy Kawasaki

Creative thinking may mean simply the realization that there's no particular virtue in doing things the way they always have been done.

Rudolf Flesch

Thinking is the hardest work there is, which is the probable reason why so few engaged in it.

Henry Ford
Charles Handy

The only reason some people get lost in thought is because it is unfamiliar territory

Paul Fix

Learning without thought is labour lost. Machines should work, People should think.

John Peers.

Unreason

The reasonable man adapts himself to the world; the unreasonable man persists in trying to adapt the world to himself. Therefore, all progress depends on the unreasonable man.

George Bernard Shaw

We are entering the Age of Unreason, a time when the future, in so many areas, is to be shaped by us and for us; a time when the only prediction that will hold true is that no prediction will hold true; a time, therefore, for bold imaginings in private life as well as public; for thinking the unlikely and doing the unreasonable.

Charles Handy

Wealth

Wealth is the product of man's capacity to think.

Ayn Rand

Wisdom

The majority believes that everything hard to comprehend must be very profound. This is incorrect. What is hard to understand is what is immature, unclear and often false. The highest wisdom is simple and passes through the brain directly into the heart.

Viktor Schauberger

The whole problem with the world is that fools and fanatics are always so certain of themselves, but wiser people so full of doubts.

Betrand Russell

Wonders

When old words die out on the tongue, new melodies break forth from the heart; and where the old tracks are lost, new country is revealed with its wonders.

Rabindranath Tagore

SOLUTIONS TO MINDXERCISES

Mindxercise 1.1

1-A, 2-F, 3-E, 4-C, 5-D, 6-B

Mindxercise 2

1. (a) Leo Gerstenzang invented cotton buds when he noticed his wife wrapping cotton on toothpicks to clean their baby's ears.
   (b) Caravan
   (c) Wheelchair, Ferris Wheel
   (d) Carburetor
2. (a) Scensational
   (b) Scensual
   (c) Scentimental
3. Look at the pairs of numbers taken from either end of the series of whole numbers from 1 to 100. They always add up to 101-100+1, 2+99, 3+98 .... 49+52, 50+51, a total of 50 pairs. Therefore, 101X50=5050 which can be done mentally within 5 seconds?
4. Hard Rock Café (b) Planet Hollywood (c) Domino Pizza
5. (a)Swatch—The Swiss watch company created Swatch as a watch fashion accessory.
   (b) Nike—Nike was the first shoe company to design shoes for specific sports like jogging, sprinting, tennis, basketball, etc.
   (c) Shandy—Shandy is a mixed drink combining beer with a sweet drink such as lemonade.
   (d) Perrier—Perrier is marketed as a high—end expensive mineral water, regarded as the Rolls-Royce of mineral drinking water.

Mindxercise 3.2

1. There are 3 faces: Father, Mother and Daughter.
   The right side of the picture shows the father with the moustache and a big nose. The center shows the mother with her eye near the big

nose and the chin and mouth next to the moustache. The face of the daughter is facing left with her chin that also forms the nose of her mother.

2. Turn the picture upside-down and you will see the face of an old lady.
3. Look at the white space between the two trees.
4. No, the man cannot be trusted. Turn the page anti—clockwise at 90 degrees and you will see the word 'Liar' in cursive writing.

Mindxercise 4.1
1. The water evaporates as it boils. Therefore there will be less hot water the longer the water boils.
2. The two girls are doubles partners.
3. 199—that is equal to the number of knock-outs before the champion is determined.
4. The anagram for "Eleven plus two" is "Twelve plus one" (b) The anagram for "The Morse Code" is "Here Come Dots" (c) The anagram for "Desperation" is "A Rope Ends It"

Mindxercise 4.2
There are several solutions to each of the problems. However, only two solutions are given to each problem in order to stimulate your creativity. Try on your own to get as many solutions as possible. Compare your solutions with those of your friends.
1. Pull the bottom match down a little and the 4 ends of the matches will form a little square. Make the number 4 (a perfect square) by moving the match on the right and place it across the ends of the two matches on the left.
2. Use a thick marker pen or a brush, cut the 2 rows and rejoin them as a single row, wrap the paper with the 2 rows of dots around a mug and you can join the 2 rows by following the curve of the mug
3. Write an 'S' in front or the number '6' behind.
4. Sun rising from mountain, a sea-wave with the sun, a woman with long hair, etc

Mindxercise 4.3
1. After giving away nine apples, the hostess gave the basket together with the last apple to the tenth child.

2. The man jumped out of the window on the ground floor of the 20-storey building.
3. You start the stopwatch at the first strike and stop the watch at the second strike. Effectively, you are measuring the time interval between the two strikes (2 sec.) which is constant. To strike 3 o'clock there will be two time intervals, which means that 4 seconds will be required. If you still do not agree, get a stop—watch ready to time the striking clock yourself.
4. Pour some food dye or other environmentally safe chemical into the lake. After a period of time, say 12 hours later, take several samples from different parts of the lake and measure the concentration of the chemical. The dilution in concentration will give an indication to the volume of the lake.
5. A dead man will not be able to rewind the tape.

Mindxercise 4.4

1. Put a thick block of ice on the pedestal. The rope will cut into the ice and can be easily removed. As the ice melts, the statue will come gently to rest on the pedestal.
2. For shampoos in bottles, the solution will be to remove the caps. Anyone trying to put the uncapped shampoos into their bags will end up with a mess. For shampoos in dispensers, have the dispensers installed above the height of the half swing-door so that they are visible to passers-by. In the case of the towels, a particular club overcame the problem by printing on the towels in clear bold letter: 'STOLEN FROM CLUB X'.
3. Reduce the size of the furniture by 20%.
4. The postman walked around the perimeter of the fence and the dog in following him will wind itself round the tree thereby reducing its reach. The postman can therefore walk safely past the dog without getting bitten.
5. The team with the building materials (Team A) sends a kite over to the team on the other side. Once the kite crosses over, Team A ties a slightly stronger material to the kite string for Team B to pull across. This process is repeated many times until the material with Team B is strong enough to pull the cables across.

Mindxercise 4.5

1. The advertisement by Amtrak, U.S.A based on the concept was a great success. The advertisement showed two windows—one looked out on clouds in the sky. Beneath the clouds was the message—'The $599 view'. The other window looked out on beautiful countryside scenery. Beneath this scene was the message—'The $79 view'. At the bottom of the ad it just said: Amtrak.

2. The TV commercial showed two women sitting side by side. One was holding a can of Pringles and the other a packet of Wise. The woman with the Pringles read out the long list of the chemical ingredients. The other woman picked up the Wise packet and read,' Wise potato chips contain potatoes, vegetable oil and salt. The TV then zoomed in on Pringles with the announcement: 'The newfangled potato chip'. It then zoomed on Wise with the announcement: "Or Wise, the oldfangled potato chip. You decide".

3. Virgin Atlantic Airways capitalized on the British Airways promotion by running an advertisement in bold capital letters: a. IT HAS ALWAYS BEEN VIRGIN'S POLICY TO ENCOURAGE YOU TO FLY TO LONDON FOR AS LITTLE AS POSSIBLE, SO ON JUNE 10 WE ENCOURAGE YOU TO FLY BRITISH AIRWAYS.
   In small print, the ad said—'As for the rest of the year, we look forward to seeing you aboard Virgin Atlantic. For the best service possible. At the lowest possible fare. 'At the bottom of the ad was the logo of Virgin Atlantic.

4. The publisher bought a colorful dinosaur balloon, inflated it with hydrogen and tied it to the top of his exhibition booth. The balloon floated above all the other booths and attracted the children's curiosity from afar. His booth stood out from the rest.

5. The company invited celebrities to try their Chupa Chups lollipops and when they did, it attracted media attention giving free publicity to the company. For instance, when the company learned that Johan Cruyff, then coach of Barcelona's soccer team, was trying to quit smoking, it generously sent him a complimentary box of Chupa Chups. Chupa's pitch fit the soccer pitch. For the rest of the season, Cruyff was rarely seen on the sideline without a lollipop in his mouth. Sales in soccer—crazy Catalonia doubled that year.

Mindxercise 6

1. The most ridiculous idea was to poke out the eyes of the workers so that they could not read. From this came the practical solution of hiring blind workers. This effectively increased productivity and the company won accolades for hiring handicapped people as well.

2. A wild idea was to spread grapes over the biscuit scrap and have people jumping and stomping them so that the grape juice will provide additional flavor to the scrap. From this idea, a connection was made between grapes and wine. The factory made liqueur biscuits out of the scrap. This new product became its most profitable line.

3. A crazy idea obtained through brainstorming was to send edible telephones to their loyal customers. The idea was logically evaluated and the practical application of this idea was to send out high quality telephone-shaped chocolates to their customers.

4. A mad idea was to deliver the seasoning to homes in a cement mixer. All that needed to be done was to dump the load of seasoning in front of the house. This triggered a connection with the way seasonings are used in homes. The company sold seasoning in shakers and the amount delivered depended on the number of shakes. Since the cement mixer has a large opening, the holes in the shaker could likewise be enlarged by 10%. This was adopted and sales immediately went up by 10%.

5. A small kid who happened to drop into the brainstorming session suggested that two dinosaurs, the T-Rex with its big mouth (who could forget them in the film, Jurassic Park?) to chase customers from the two adjoining shops into their center shop. The owner made a connection between the T-Rex's big mouth and a big shop entrance. The result was that the shop—owner put out a sign 'Main Entrance' in front of the shop capitalizing on the sales promotion on either side.

Mindxercise 7

1. The nurses bandage the teddy bears and told the children that they (the bears) were sick and needed to stay in the hospital for treatment. This has the additional benefit of the children treating the teddy bears with greater tenderness.

2. Mr. Earl Dickson, who was working for Johnson & Johnson, invented pre-prepared bandage with a gauze invented that caught the notice of the company. The bandage Band-Aid became a highly profitable product for Johnson & Johnson.

3. Stone saw a connection between the process for making his paper cigarette holders and an artificial drinking straw. By wrapping a long thin strip of paper around a pencil, he created the first artificial drinking straw.

4. Morse drew on the connection with the relay horses to come out with a relay system for the transmission of telegraph signals. Basically, at each relay station, the power of the signal is boosted considerably before sending over to the next relay station and the process is repeated at each station.

5. George de Mestral designed a unique, two-sided fastener, one side with stiff hooks like the burrs and the other side with soft loops like the fabric of his pants. He called the invention 'velcro' a combination of the word velour and crochet, a modern fastener that is used in a variety of products that need fastening—bags, shoes, clothes, etc

6. The woman named her dog "naked" and took her for a walk in the busy shopping area in compliance with her promise.

Mindxercise 8
1. The farmer's daughter accepted the landlord's offer. She picked up a pebble from the bag and pretended to carelessly drop it. She apologized for her clumsiness but said that it did not matter since the color of the remaining pebble in the bag would indicate what she had picked. Thus she took advantage of the landlord's trick against him and won freedom from debt for her father.

2. John C. Kullen founded DG Books Worldwide Inc. that is best known for publishing the world's best selling . . . For Dummies series which has to date more than 19 million copies in print with translations in 32 languages.

3. Anita Roddick founded the highly successful Bodyshop line of body—care products and specialty shops selling them based on primitive and native plus environmentally—friendly formulations.

4. The shoes are for training in mountain—climbing to prepare the climber for the actual trip.

5. Habitat, a subsidiary of IKEA adopted the "morning after look" for its latest catalogue of furniture products. The catalog shows scenes of reality in homes—models in wrinkled clothes lie face down on an untidy pile of pillows, seemingly passed out in an unmade bed,. crumpled dish towels left to dry on an exposed radiator, unwashed

cups and saucers, etc. Get the picture? Now guess what happened? The catalogue attracted attention and the catalogue sold more than a million copies in the UK alone.

Mindxercise 9

1. Cut a small hole in piece of paper, hold it close to the TV, then poke your finger through it to push the TV.
2. Water
3. Paper lantern
4. Frog
5. Light the match under a glass of water
6. Toss the ball vertically upwards
7. Human (baby: crawling, toddler to adult: walking, old folks walking with walking sticks)
8. No idea (No Eye Deer)
9. Two (2) oranges
10. The weight of the petrol burned in crossing the bridge in travelling 3 km will be more than enough to offset the weight of the bird.

SUGGESTED READING ON CREATIVITY

Parents and Teachers
- Dr. YKK (Yew Kam Keong, Ph.D), Nurturing Creative Children—30 Simple and Practical Tips for you to discover the Joys of Parenthood, Mindbloom
- Stevanne Aueback, Dr. Toy's Smart Play—How to raise a Child with a high P.Q, St. Martin's Griffin
- Chuck Moorman & Nancy Weber, Teacher Talk—What it really Means, Institute for Personal Power
- Chuck Moorman & Thomas Haller, The 10 Commandments Parenting With a Purpose, Personal Power Press
- Steve Biddulph, The Secret of Happy Children, HarperCollins Publishers
- Glenn Doman & Janet Doman, How To Multiply Your Baby's Intelligence, Amery Publishing Group
- Jamilah Samian, Cool Mum, Super Dad, Truewealth
- Don Campbell, The Mozart Effect for Children, Black Thistle Press
  A good start to light and easy reading on creativity, less than 200 pages, I would recommend the following:
- Roger von Oech, A Whack on the Side of the Head, Warner Bros. Inc.
- John Adair, The Art of Creative Thinking, Talbot Adair Press
- Jack Foster, How to Get Ideas, Berrett-Koehler Publishers, Inc.
- Robert Alan Black, Broken Crayons, Cre8ng Places Press
- Tom Wujec, Five Star Mind (Games and Puzzles to Stimulate Your Creativity), Doubleday ·Jim Wheeler, The Power of Innovative Thinking (Let new ideas lead you to success), Advantage Quest Publication

GENERAL READING

- Malcolm Gladwell, Blink: The Power of Thinking Without Thinking, Back Ray Books · Kishore Mahbubano, Can Asians Think?, Times Books International
- John Howkins, The Creative Economy, Penguin Group
- James M. Higgins, 101 Creative Problem Solving Techniques, New Management Publishing, Co. Inc.
- John D. Bransford and Barry S. Stein, The Ideal Problem Solver (A Guide for Improving Thinking, Learning, and Creativity), W. H. Freeman & Co.
- Ng Aik Huang, Liberating the Creative Spirit, Pearson
- Dilip Mukerjea, Braindancing, The Brainwave Press
- Dilip Mukerjea, Brainfinity, Oxord University Press
- Dilip Mukerjea, Superbrain, Oxord University Press
- Peter Drucker, Innovation and Entrepreneurship, Harper Business
- Michael Michalko, Cracking Creativity (the Secrets of Creative Genius), Ten Speed Press
- Win Winger and Richard Poe, The Einstein Factor, Prima Publishing
- Arthur van Gundy, Training Your Creative Mind, Prentice Hall
- Leonard S. M. Yong, The Joy of Creativity, Incotrends (M) Sdn. Bhd.
- Roger B. Yepsen, Jr., How to Boost Your Brain Power, Rodale Press, Inc.
- Arthur van Gundy, Creative Problem Solving (A Guide for Trainers and Management), Quorum Books
- Michael Hewitt-Gleeson, Software for the Brain, Heinemann Asia
- J. Geoffrey Rawlinson, Creative Thinking and Brainstorming, Gower Publishing Co. Ltd.
- Tony Buzan, Make the Most of Your Mind, Pan Books

- Tony Buzan, Use Both Sides of Your Brain: New Mind-Mapping Techniques, Plume
- Edward de Bono, Thinking Course, BBC Books
- Alex Osborn, Applied Imagination, Charles Scribner's Sons
- Alex Osborn, Your Creative Power (How to Use Your Imagination to Brighten Life, to get Ahead), Motorola University Press
- James M. Higgins, Escape from the Maze (9 Steps to Personal Creativity), New Management Publishing Company
- Joel Arthur Barker, Paradigms (The Business of Discovering the Future), HarperBusiness
- Michael LeBoeuf, Creative Thinking (How to generate Ideas and Turn Them into Successful Reality), Judy Piatkus (Publishers) Ltd.
- Richard Forbes, The Creative Problem Solver Handbook, Solutions through Innovation

RECOMMENDED READING FOR MANAGERS AND BUSINESS EXECUTIVES

- Dr. YKK (Yew Kam Keong, PhD), Creative Business Challenges: Innovative Business Solutions, Mindbloom Consulting
- Jan Verloop, Insight in Innovation (Managing Innovation by Understanding the Laws of Innovations), Elsevier Inc.
- W. Chan Kim, Renée Mauborgne, Blue Ocean Strategy: How to Create Uncontested Market Space and Make Competition Irrelevant, Reed Elsevier Inc.
- Richard Florida, The Rise of the Creative Class: And How It's Transforming Work, Leisure, Community and Everyday Life, Basic Books
- Doug Hall and Tom Peters, Jump Start Your Business Brain: Ideas, Advice, and Insights for Immediate Marketing and Innovation Success, Emmis Books
- Donalee Markus, Lindsey Markus, and Pat Taylor, Retrain Your Business Brain: Outsmart the Corporate Competition Kaplan Business
- Jane Henry, Creativity and Perception in Management, Sage Publications Ltd
- Harvard Business Review, The Innovative Enterprise, Harvard Business School Publishing Corporation
- Brian Clegg, Creativity and Innovation for Managers, Butterworth—Heinemann
- Bobbi Porter, Quantum Learning for Business, Dell Publishing
- Gregory P. Smith, The New Leader (Bringing Creativity to the Workplace), St. Lucie Press
- Min Basadur, The Power of Innovation, Pitman Publishing

- John Kao, Jamming (The Art & Discipline of Business Creativity), HarperCollins Business
- Alan West, Innovation Strategy, Prentice Hall
- Michael Michalko, Cracking Creativity: The Secrets of Creative Genius, Ten Speed Press
- Michael Michalko, Thinkertoys (Handbook of Business Creativity), Advantage Quest Publications
- Alan G. Robinson & Sam Stern, Corporate Creativity, Berrett— Koehler Publishers, Inc.
- Matthew J. Kiernan, Get Innovative or Get Dead (Building Competitive Companies for the 21st Century), Douglas & Mc Intyre Ltd.,
- Robin E. McDermott, Raymond J. Mikulak, Michael R. Beuregard, Employee Driven Quality (Releasing the Creative Spirit of Your Organization through Suggestion Systems), Quality Resources
- Marsh Fisher, The IdeaFisher (How to Land the Big Idea—and other Secrets of Creativity in Business), Advantage Quest Publications
- Camille Cates Barnett, The Creative Manager, International City Management Association
- Stephen R. Grossman, Ruce E. Rodgers and Beverly R. Moore, Innovation, Inc. (Unlocking Creativity in the Workplace), Wordware Publishing, Inc.
- Neville Smith and Murray Ainsworth, Ideas Unlimited (The Mindmix Approach to Innovative Management), Nelson Publishers
- John Emmerling, It takes One (How to Create the Right Idea—and then make It Happen), Simon & Schuster
- Michael Ray and Rochelle Myers, Creativity in Business, Doubleday & Co., Inc.
- Guy Kawasaki, How to Drive Your Competition Crazy, Hyperion

RECOMMENDED CREATIVITY WEBSITES

THE CREATIVITY SITE
This is my website. http://www.mindbloom.net
Below are comments from one of my website visitors:
Jam—packed with information. Check it out to find out how you can:
- Increase your ability to find the solutions to any problem that you may have
- Exercise your mind to keep it in tip—top shape at no cost!
- Increase your Intelligent Quotient in a few simple steps!
- Learn how great personalities of the past have made your life easier by using nothing more than just their minds!
- Bring up children with the respect you deserve!
- Make your children smarter, more responsive and not take things for granted.

And much, much, more!
LEMELSON-MIT PROGRAM
http://web.mit.edu/invent/w-main.html
This is incredible and the best website I have found on the history of inventions. It was created by the Massachusetts Institute of Technology (MIT).
INVENTION HELP YOU
http://www.invention-help.com/
It is a complete help resource and a portal to the world of inventing that can help you through your voyage of invention.
CREATIVITY FOR LIFE
http://www.creativityforlife.com/
This website has many interesting articles exploring creativity in our everyday lives.
GLOBAL IDEAS BANK

http://www.globalideasbank.org/site/home/
The ideas bank contains thousands of ideas from every corner of the globe.

BROKEN CRAYONS

http://www.cre8ng.com

Broken Crayons is the web site by Robert Alan Black—speaker and author on creativity and innovation. This site is home to the weekly Creativity Challenges posted to several Creativity discussion lists.

CREATIVE IDEAS

http://www.creativeideas.org.uk/

A free resource for exploring creativity & innovation within business and society. It employs an innovative approach using Musical Performance in Creativity Training.

ENCHANTED MIND

http://www.enchantedmind.com

This is a colourful, well-designed site with a great deal of information on creativity techniques and inspiring articles, puzzles including some interactive Java puzzles.

THE CREATIVE EDUCATION FOUNDATION

http://www.creativeeducationfoundation.org/

It empowers you to define opportunities, identify ideas and implement solutions. Its mission is to help individuals, organizations and communities transform themselves as they confront real—world challenges.

INNOVATION TOOLS

http://www.innovationtools.com

Run by Chuck Frey, this excellent site provides busy executives with a valuable collection of tools, ideas and resources, designed to help them be more creative in their day—to—day work.

DIRECTED CREATIVITY

http://www.directedcreativity.com

The Directed Creativity cycle proposed on this site consists of Preparation, Imagination, Development and Action. The site has a comprehensive collection of creativity techniques and uses a lot of mind maps to good effect.

MIND TOOLS

http://www.mindtools.com

Techniques for Memory, Creativity, Skills for high performance living and practical psychology.

IM-BOOT
http://www.im-boot.org/
A great place to get started when trying to find out how different people in different countries tackle the innovation dilemma.
ODDYSSEY OF THE MIND
http://www.odysseyofthemind.org
The site promotes creative team—based problem solving in a school program for students from kindergarten through college. The program helps students learn divergent thinking and problem solving skills.

CREATIVITY AND INNOVATION LIBRARY
http://www.jpb.com/creative/
Provides lots of free articles, papers and tools to help you and your company be more creative and innovative. You can subscribe to Report 103, a fortnightly newsletter on creativity, imagination, ideas and innovation in business.
EDWARD DE BONO
http://www.edwdebono.com
Edward de Boon's web site gives information on most of de Bono's work in the teaching of creativity: Six Hats, Lateral Thinking and the CoRT program for schools.
CPSI—CREATIVE PROBLEM SOLVING INSTITUTE
http://www.cef-cpsi.org
Home of the Creative Education Foundation, and organiser of CPSI—the Creative Problem Solving Institute.
WHAT A GREAT IDEA!
http://www.whatagreatidea.com
This is Charles "Chic" Thompson's site. Chic's passion is inspiring executives,
MBA students and children to be "curious first . . . critical second" while problem solving.
CREATIVITY OUT OF THE BOX
http://www.isixsigma.com/tt/out_of_the_box/
It tells us what creativity and creative thinking are and how creative thinking techniques work. Articles on Creativity techniques and creative tools for problem solving as well as puzzles to exercise the creative mind.
CREATIVITY AND INNOVATION-IDEAFLOW BLOG
http://ideaflow.corante.com/

IdeaFlow is an interesting innovation Blog with contributions running the gamut from creativity puzzles, to conference updates, to interesting innovation websites and articles to random thoughts on innovation by the participants.
CREATIVITY POOL
http://www.creativitypool.com
This is an inspiring knowledge base full of creative and original ideas. It's the home of future innovation and tomorrow's most (in) famous inventions.
CENTER FOR SUSTAINABLE DESIGN
http://www.cfsd.org.uk/smart-know-net/
The Sustainable Marketing Knowledge Network (Smart: Know—Net) is an online resource that exists to bring together the world of marketing and sustainability.
BUSINESSWEEK ONLINE
http://www.businessweek.com
This online magazine has an Innovation Section which is an incredible source of information on the latest innovation updates.
CREATIVE QUOTATIONS
http://www.bemorecreative.com
A comprehensive site to look for quotations on creativity, well organized into specific categories.

PROFILE OF AUTHOR DR. YKK

Dr. YKK (Yew Kam Keong, Ph. D) is an acknowledged *Distinguished Talent* on creativity, a former international creativity adviser to Lego and a member of Mensa. He has been described as an energetic speaker, a provocative mind unzipper, an entertaining laughter guru, a masterful story—teller and bestselling author all rolled into one. This together with his wide international exposure and diverse work experience enable him to connect well with his audience and readers.

Dr YKK delivers tailored keynote speeches, conducts creativity and business innovations training sessions as well as facilitates problem-solving and idea generating sessions for the corporate, public, professional and business organisations.

He is married with four children. Constantly seeking new and challenging experiences, he lives a life of adventure that includes skydiving, scuba—diving, mountain-climbing, water-skiing, theme-park rides and whitewater rafting.

Dr. YKK can be contacted at:
E-mail: DrYKK@mindbloom.net or yewkk@yahoo.com
Skype: dryewkk
Website: www.mindbloom.net